Gardening Notes
from a
Late Bloomer

Gardening Notes from a Late Bloomer

CLARE HASTINGS

with drawings by Osbert Lancaster

PIMPERNEL
PRESS LTD
www.pimpernelpress.com

To Calypso, James and Hendricks

Pimpernel Press Limited
www.pimpernelpress.com

Gardening Notes from a Late Bloomer
© Pimpernel Press Limited 2018
Text © Clare Hastings 2018
Drawings by Osbert Lancaster © Clare Hastings
Endpapers and design by Becky Clarke

A catalogue record for this book is available from the
British Library.

Typeset in Bodoni Twelve ITC

ISBN 978-1-910258-98-9
Printed and bound in China
by C&C Offset Printing Company Limited

9 8 7 6 5 4 3 2 1

Contents

1

Gardening Beyond the Grave

I 'M NOT DEAD YET. In fact I woke up this morning feeling quite chipper. I glanced out of the window at a large topiary snail, which is making slow but determined progress up to the cottage door, and thought about you (which of course I do a lot) and felt a frisson of panic. What if I were to be struck down before elevenses on the B4009? Apart from the obvious gaps this would leave, I realized that I needed to leave you a handbook about the garden. For you the countryside is the pathway leading from the car park to the cottage door, to be completed, collar turned up, on the run, but I'm not giving up. I know you see, that it really is in your DNA. Your grandmother was a gardening writer, and used to say that the one thing connecting our dysfunctional family was a love of plants, which I still think is true. I was a very late starter, too much to do, too little time, and I lacked confidence.

I would look at other gardens and gaze in wonder at the borders and the planting. I used to think that you needed to be rather academic to garden, with a sound knowledge of Latin names and experience of scale – and maybe some knowledge of how to analyse soil would be handy too. This meant that I was rather nervous around plants, always wondering if they should be paired together or kept apart. Bare beds were a source of panic and pruning a thing best left to the grown-ups. I longed to just be told what to do. Then I had a light bulb moment. I realized that although it would be nice to be a proper plantsman, I'm not, and it's never going to happen now, but the great thing is *it doesn't matter*. A garden is life, filled with ups and downs. There are moments when you want to divorce it and other times you can sit alongside it forever.

The garden you are going to inherit is a terribly higgledy-piggledy cottage garden, but one where with love and care on certain days when the light pings through a tree or a plant behaves itself, you will find yourself filled with an unbelievable shot of happiness. So here are some gardening life notes, to help you up the path, and I absolutely promise I won't be a ghost by the tree peony (the tall thing with large seed pods) judging your efforts. Think of me as a contented spirit peeking out, wishing the plants well and giving an evil eye to the slugs, snails, pigeons, moles, magpies, deer, greenfly, whitefly and all the rest of the pests who will be waiting, mandibles, beaks and claws at the ready.

Gardening from beyond the grave – bring it on.

2

Who's Who
in the Garden

WELL ME OF COURSE, **CLARE**, mother to **Calypso**, grandmother to **Hendricks and mother-in-law to James**. When I'm not in the garden I still think about plants. I am a compulsive tidier, which is not a good thing to be if you have a garden, as it will never, ever be totally tidy – unless of course you own the paved patio type, which you can sweep with a new broom every day. I have had to learn not to worry about this; there really aren't enough hours in the day. I do still prefer it when the hedges are clipped and the tools are neatly stacked, I feel at peace. Weeds do not instil a sense of calm – indeed on a windy day when the seed pods are ripe, the reverse. I am the kind of person who instead of waiting nicely at the bus stop, can be spotted deadheading a tub of forgotten pansies over a stranger's wall. We all have our issues.

NICK, long-term partner to Clare and the man who wields the strimmer. Nick is still adjusting to flowers; he prefers vegetables, which appeal to both his stomach and his innate love of straight lines. He is an executive pruner and scythe sharpener. Unlike Clare, Nick knows when he has had enough gardening and retires without a backward glance to his man shed. He is also the best person to consult on removing a rabbit or potting a squirrel. He does not see nature through the soft-focus lenses of an urbanite, but with the hard head of a man who will not be parted from his broad beans.

TED, the dog; well adjusted to life in London parks, he finds the rigours of brambles and the height of wheat in the country a bit of a trial. He perks up when the grass is a sensible length and he can make steady unimpeded progress. He is Nick's constant companion and lover of a bumpy ride in an ancient Land Rover.

BEAN, best friend, Nick's 'extra wife' and my gardening chum. Everyone needs a gardening friend to compete, share and bounce ideas off. Bean comes to the garden a lot, and I go to hers. We know about the same amount, but on different stuff. Bean's garden is just lovely, and although it is very different from mine we are both heading in the same direction style-wise, which is an important element in a gardening mate.

MALCOLM, the mower, grass cutter extraordinaire. Thank God for Malcolm, as pre M. mowing nearly did for us.

'GOD DAD' has been in and out of the garden for ever. He is hopeless when it comes to plants, so don't look for help there, but very willing to move large, unwieldy objects. He started off the rockery, so you get the idea. Book him well in advance, he can be somewhat elusive.

GRANNY, gardening writer and lover of any kind of plants. She was just as happy looking for herbs on a Greek hillside as judging at Chelsea (actually probably more so). She loved our cottage and the garden, and of course a lot of the plants are here because of her influence. Granny expected me to learn by osmosis, which I did a bit, but it wasn't until I became really hands on that I could actually call any plant by its name.

3

Do You Remember
in the Garden?

THE OTHER DAY I WAS READING about the demise of the 'front garden'– how sad. I love front gardens. I also love those small strips of garden you see in villages, where the owner has commandeered the verge in front of their house and filled in the extra foot with cuttings and flowers. Unlike a driveway, which isn't very thrilling, a front garden gives you a glimpse into a life. A garden is a wonderful aid to memory and should be filled with memories, not cars. Ours is. Everywhere I look I am reminded of a day, an event, a lunch. When I glance out of the window at the concrete bird bath I think 'junk shop', where Bean and I have both spent more hours than is good for us vying for treasures. Every time we sit around the slate table I think 'hernia', which is what 'god dad' got attempting to lift the top single-handed from the roof of his car. Obviously I'm not allowed to forget that incident – ever. There is nothing like an operation to cement events.

There have been quite a lot of funerals in the garden. Hamsters in small boxes are buried under hedges; Porridge and Harris, our previous dogs, have been laid to rest in their favourite garden spots with a mowing stone to mark the grave, and granny is scattered under the hazel from where she can clock the family (and equally we can keep an eye on her). I remember looking out of the back window one morning (in the pre-hazel days), to spot her grovelling in the back garden with a bunch of bare twigs, which she was stuffing into an uncultivated patch of earth. At the time I thought she had lost the plot but now I have a huge shrub of dogwood (*Cornus alba*), the fruit of her three-minute labour. I have cuttings from Paxos, hollyhock seeds from Morocco, scented narcissi from best friend Bean, and I am still digging up slightly sad spoons and forks from your childhood camps. Plants are a great way to create memories. A cutting from a friend's garden is as good as a photograph and will always spark a reminder of the time of year, the occasion, and sometimes even the weather.

We have argued and sobbed round the borders and done a lot of laughing too. I certainly won't forget your wedding in a hurry, the front garden awash with about a hundred catering cans, and Nick rather grumpily spraying them gold and silver to use as vases. He tackled the triumphal arch with much more enthusiasm as it involved pole collecting in the Land Rover (a man's task). Made from regenerated ash poles, it now embellishes the entrance to the vegetable garden. The arch was indeed a triumph and looks completely at home in the new spot. It still sports a wedding sign, which is wearing remarkably well. The arch weighed a ton and required local help to get it back from the wedding field (we decided not to ask 'god dad'). I am growing a rose through it, as well as an everlasting sweet pea which self-seeded and is winding its way up to the top (doing rather better than the rose, which is typical).

The topiary snail by the front path started off as a round box ball, a birthday gift from our friends Mog and Dick. Later I planted a wire frame of a pecking chicken beside it and filled that with another box plant. Malcolm the mower decided he really didn't take to the chicken and knocked the head off so many times that it became 'the headless chicken'. Fast forward a few years and the two box plants linked up. Nick then had a creative moment with the kitchen scissors and now we have a snail. Even that has problems, as Nick got the shell swirl the wrong way round and was so cross when he noticed that he is growing it out to start again. Some shapes are not meant to be. I always love gardens with mad topiary balls but on our plot they grow so slowly that Hendricks will be an old man before they do anything verging on exciting.

There are new memories in progress. The 'Hendricks Walk' is taking shape in a previous bit of scrub garden. It started off being the 'woodland walk' but then we chopped down all the woody bits so it was due a name change before it was even finished.

Plant scented flowers. There is no point in a rose that doesn't smell. An old adage, but scent really does prompt memories and really, if it is a choice between a flower with scent and one without there isn't a contest.

I have loads of tales to tell that revolve around the garden, but you do too. One of your favourite childhood reads was a wonderful book by Ruth Craft, *The Winter Bear*. It tells the tale of three children who go on a walk and spot a bear wedged in a tree: 'A bit damp, a bit leafy, in need of repair, but still an excellent bear'. It was indeed an extraordinary moment when your very own winter bear turned up in the hazel. How he got there and where he came from nobody knows, but you remember finding him lodged in the branches as if it were yesterday. Stick whittling was excellent fun. The soft wood from the hazel is just the best if you want to peel patterns and shapes into the bark and your personalized sticks made very good gifts (we've still got a couple) and also kept you engaged for hours, as did gathering seeds and grasses for collages. Hooray for craft!

Some Scented Flowers and Shrubs You Simply Can't do Without

PINKS There are loads of different ones but only buy the scented. There are some unscented ones that are perfectly pretty, but that, as in life, is not enough.

JASMINE We have a summer variety that is planted with the climbing roses over the arch at the back. I don't think I am making the most of it. The scent is delicate and it is an easy climber.

LAVENDER I prefer the English varieties. 'Hidcote' is the most compact and the best for edging the steps.

PHILADELPHUS 'BELLE ETOILE' This is planted round the back and fills the air with perfume. It flowers in the early summer, and every garden should have one.

HONEYSUCKLE We planted one by the front door and on a warm day you can stand and enjoy a waft when the door is open.

ROSES You can't have enough. We don't and I want more.

DAPHNE ODORA A shrub with a variegated leaf. I have just planted three of these (on Bean's advice) on a rocky slope, which previously housed nettles. I am quite excited, as I believe the scent is delicious.

SCENTED NARCISSI Bean has given me loads. They not only look lovely, they also smell divine.

SWEET PEAS Don't forget to plant these every year. Nothing beats them as a cut flower, the more you pick the more they grow, producing flower after flower. As with pinks there are loads of different types but the smell is the point. I have grown them in a tub too, as once you have started them on an upward path they don't take up much room.

SCENTED PELARGONIUMS These make the perfect pot plants and the leaves can smell of anything from nutmeg to oranges. 'Attar of Roses' is one of my favourites (and I have *a lot* of favourites); you can use the leaves in tea. They are extraordinarily easy to grow and maintain. Just take off the dead leaves and hack them back if they get too large. I could do a whole terrace with them and never get bored.

HERBS, HERBS AND MORE HERBS You can never have enough and rubbing the leaves as you totter past is an instant energizer.

4

Wildlife
in the Garden

Y ES, I KNOW, I AM ALWAYS WHINGING about
the amount of wildlife that seems to maraud through
our borders. Only the other day I came upon a pheasant
destroying a huge patch of crocus, pecking off the newly-
opened heads; while a couple of hours earlier a Muntjac deer
was spotted trotting through the Hendricks Walk and pausing
to browse a new rose. It is war, but I wouldn't have it any other
way. If you are positioned on the edge of a field, in a cottage with
what amounts to a nest as a roof, you really do have to learn to
live with it and so we do.

Every year, after the harvest, just as you are snuggling down
for a cosy night, you will hear the scrabbling of little feet
right above your head. This is the start of a mouse migration.
Whatever you do, and however carefully the roof is netted
they will squeeze into the roof void. If the feet start to sound
like hobnail boots then it is Ratty, or if the sound is similar

to small children on a trampoline then you have Squirrel. I personally am not too fond of small furries penetrating the property, especially when the feet are followed up by the sound of teeth tearing into the rafters, so you will need to harden up. Mice have, on odd occasions, got in the house (once eating through the alarm wire), and while I have never caught a rat in a trap (and we have tried), we are quite successful with mice. Nick has to prise the bodies off the spikes; I can't quite cope. They are partial to chocolate and peanut butter (no palm oil, that's me, Mouse doesn't care). Getting access to them in the roof (note plural as there is never just one mouse) was slightly problematical so Nick creatively constructed a small access door in the ceiling, which is our poison point. There are a couple of nails so you can lodge the poison blocks in position. On a good night you can hear them chomping away at their deadly treat. We are never quite sure if we are baiting more in with this process, but rodents are not good for thatch so they have to go (sorry). Jackdaws have fallen down the chimney a couple of times causing havoc but I think we have managed to stop that with hats on the chimney pots.

There are some animals that I have only spotted once or twice and I treasure the memories. When you were small I had an Attenborough moment and saw a mole scuttling round the hazel in the front garden. Luckily I had on my gardening gloves, and the mole was not the brightest and I actually caught it. We put him in your hamster's plastic travelling box for observation. He was a treat with his paddle feet and soft coat. I set him free across the road. To pay me back for this indignation his relatives have been plaguing me ever since. This year, to really rub my nose in it, they have dug underneath the sonic mole repellent, leaving a fine tilth hill around the stick. Disrespect or what? Another gadget for the bin and, by the way, I have no faith in sonic mouse plugs either. The clicking is a human rather than a rodent irritant.

I have only seen hedgehogs maybe once or twice; they are such shy, endearing souls. Once I looked out of the window to see a weasel doing his dance of death. It was the most extraordinary display of athleticism and I long for a rerun. Apparently they mesmerize their prey, and I was indeed mesmerized. Stoats sometimes dash up and down under the front hedge in a mad way. I'm not sure what they are up to but they do it at a speed that would leave Usain Bolt standing and they are completely fascinating.

Recently Nick and I spotted a newt under one of your log wedding seats – this was another first – and a badger was caught in the automatic spotlight a foot from the cottage but luckily this one was just passing through. Spring is their time to wreak havoc. One sunny morning you will throw open the bedroom curtains and gasp. Yes, the whole of the front garden will be reduced to chaos with holes dug everywhere. This is Badger, snouting out leatherjacket larvae (aka daddy-long-legs), which live in the grass roots. You can water the grass with nematodes – microscopic worms which enter the bodies of the little leatherjackets, infecting them with a deadly bacterial disease. This is all blissfully organic apparently: no leatherjackets, no badgers.

Different nematodes can be used for doing in all sorts of pests from slugs to vine weevils (don't ask). The nematodes arrive in boxes stating they are 'live' and must be placed immediately in the fridge, which makes me rather anxious. They are microscopic and hidden in what appears to be sawdust, but they are clearly trained assassins. I have visions of them breaking out of their packaging. I don't use them for the lawn (I just fill up the holes with soil and scatter a few grass seeds over the top), but I have applied them in the vegetable garden around the lettuce to intimidate the slugs. If you start trying to manage everything, it never stops and is rather expensive.

Nick is rabbit and squirrel controller and pots them from out of the bedroom window. It is usually dawn, and makes for a somewhat startling and eccentric awakening, as the noise is shattering and Nick is naked. You should probably train up James or baby Hendricks as gardening and rabbits are not partners. I know you have house bunnies, but it might help to think of wild rabbits as an alien life form. Squirrel digs up all the bulbs given half a chance. Indeed I had planned a naturalized area for crocus down the front path but I was just squirrel feeding so I have given up. I know I could cover the bulbs with wire but sometimes it is simpler to admit defeat and squirrels are as bad as deer for eating new shoots. My recently planted pittosporum hedge looks a bit bare around the base, as they have had fun stripping back the bark. It is not the look I had planned.

Muntjac and roe deer wander by from time to time but they are very shy and don't cause too many dramas. A rose might get an occasional pruning but a look from Nick gets them moving pretty speedily.

I do hope Hendricks will see loads of garden animals. There are often small green frogs hiding in the cool of the rockery under the ivy, it's an excellent spot to begin a garden safari.

5

Eating
the Garden

Y OU SAY 'FOODIE', I SAY 'GREEDY'. There are
some trees in the garden that are good for greedies.
Our Victoria plum is the winner. Even in a bad year the
branches hang to the ground laden with huge purple fruits.
The fruit is ideal for sugar-packed treats – jam, crumbles
and chutney – and you can even appear generous by donating
sackfuls to all and sundry. This year I noticed there has been
an uptake in plum moths. The tiny, wriggly grubs nestle inside
round the stone, wreaking havoc if you leave them too long.
I just wash them out under the tap and carry on cooking (I
hate prissie cooks). You could buy pheromone traps to hang
in the tree (the male moth is lured to a sticky death, leaving
unrequited females). I haven't bothered, so lucky is the plum
moth that lands in our garden.

I am not a good tree pruner. I get too emotionally involved
with the severed branches. Nick is a kill or cure type of pruner,

leaving the tree with an appearance of a large stump. Plum trees should be tackled in spring or summer when they are less prone to suffer from infections. This year Nick had a major go at the greengage in early September; as I like to follow instructions, this was nearly an early grave moment. If the gage survives, try to collect the delicious fruit before the wasps. This means picking them while they are still slightly hard and letting them ripen in the house, which they do pretty speedily. If the wasps get a sniff at the sweet sticky juice, it is all over bar a lot of shouting.

Every garden should have a couple of fruit trees. We inherited four (planted too closely together), and put in a couple ourselves. You probably remember when we bought our 'John Downie' crab apple – you named it Clarence and it stands at rather a jaunty angle. In fact all the trees we planted are on the lean, so learn from our mistakes and stake any new trees properly so they can't rock in the wind before the roots have had a chance to dig in. Clarence produces masses of somewhat scabby crabs, but what they lack in appearance they make up for in taste, producing the most beautiful clear orange jelly.

I have also started to pickle walnuts. I have found you only need to do this every three years, as there are only so many walnuts you can consume, but they are a brilliant addition to any ragout or gravy, giving a sharp kick to the sauce and adding richness. Pick the walnuts when they are green. Start to look at the tree in mid-June when the outer skins are still very soft and follow the recipe on page 26. They are great to eat with cheese too, adding a certain cachet to a supper.

Quince cheese is another foodie treat, but you have to cook the quinces for ages, so I have abandoned this *pro tem* although I do enjoy the process of wrapping up the jelly squares into parcels with greaseproof paper. I have a new plan for quince this year. While on holiday in South Africa we saw a quince tree bedecked with large bottles attached by wire to the branches, the emerging fruit inside the glass. Apparently they leave the quince to swell up and mature inside the bottle, then detach the bottle and fill it with gin or vodka. *Voilà* quince gin and nobody knows how the quince got in there! Obviously this is a slow, mindful present but maybe it will catch on. I shall give it a go.

I have always liked pickled onions. You either do or you don't, and a couple of small jars look pretty in the cupboard. It is a good way to use shallots (cover them in boiling water for ten minutes first as it makes them a doddle to peel), and you can add any very small onions to the mix. I used to fill giant Kilner jars, but they start to look a bit sad and sticky halfway through the year so now I use small jars.

Autumn is a busy time in the preserving world and you mustn't hang about, the fruit won't. A couple of weekends of graft should result in a cupboard filled with loveliness for the year. There is an idea floated around that you should give away the fruits of your labour but I never seem to make enough to be that indulgent. With your sugar phobia perhaps you won't bother or maybe you could just make it and then donate it to anyone with a full set of veneers. I wouldn't like to see a jam ban and throwing away fruit seems a terrible shame.

Over the years I have bottled beans (emulating those jars you see in French delicatessens) and plums. The plums, marinated in sugar syrup, were in a huge jar. They sat for twenty years at the top of cupboard waiting for the Armageddon moment but then, one weekend when I wasn't around, Nick and his friend James found them and ate the lot (no consequences, which was a result). I miss my plums. I was very proud of the fact that over the years they had kept their colour and never went furry.

Early in spring pay attention to the patch of rhubarb in the front garden. It is a pretty pink colour and looks much more wholesome than the forced stuff. It cooks in a minute (a sugar fest again, sorry). I have a delicious tart recipe, which is so light that two people can easily knock it off in a sitting, but it is meant for four. Rhubarb leaves are poisonous so don't chop them in salad but twist them off and chuck them on the manure heap. The rhubarb patch has been going for forty years. It gets covered with weeds every year but it never seems to mind and just bounces up again. Don't let it go to seed. Chop off the very obvious bulbous heads if you see one come up. In the winter clean all the old leaves away so the crown of the rhubarb is exposed, it gets the stalks up and running for next season. Oh yes – very important – don't pick but *pull* rhubarb up by holding the base and giving a sharp tug, so it doesn't snap off. Too much info – I promise it is a truly simple plant!

DON'T FORGET IT IS FUN TO FORAGE

I have used the tops of young nettles on several occasions when I have run out of vegetables. They steam beautifully and, with a bit of butter, taste very similar to spinach. They also make a very tasty soup. Obviously they are sting-free at the point of eating but wear gloves to pick them and only take the young fresh ones. The sting is in the hairs and is produced by the presence of formic acid, which is destroyed by washing or boiling.

Sloes are a great free food, and are a blissful addition to gin. As good as (Nick thinks better than) a cracker for Christmas cheer. Blackberries are a clear winner, and the jelly makes an unusual addition to a joint of lamb.

Once you get your eye in everything starts to turn into food.

Recipes

NETTLE PESTO

Pick the tops of the nettles in the spring when they are at their tastiest. Wash well. Dunk a big handful into boiling water until wilted (a minute, no more). Drain. Blend with freshly grated Parmesan, chopped garlic, a handful of pine nuts and a good glug of olive oil. Whizz until smooth. Spoon over freshly cooked pasta and mix in well. Nettles are rich in vitamins C and A and are very good for you.

CRAB APPLE JELLY

2 kg (4½ lb) crab apples
Rind of 2 lemons
Sugar (preserving or, if you haven't got that, ordinary)
    450 g (16 oz) for every 600 ml (21 fl oz) of juice

Wash and halve the crabs. Leave in all the pips, peel, core and stalks. Place in a pan with the lemon rind. Cover with water and heat, keeping it at a rolling boil. Once cooked to a pulp, transfer to a jelly bag hanging over a large bowl (this is a two-man job, as the pulp is super hot). It will strain through pretty quickly. You are allowed to squeeze the pulp a bit but don't overdo it or the jelly will be cloudy. Measure the juice, return to a clean pan and add the sugar. Start off on a low heat to dissolve the sugar, then bring it up to a boil. You should reach setting point after about 10 minutes. Skim off any foam with a metal spoon. Ladle into sterilized, warm jars. I add a stick of rosemary when the jelly has started to set, which makes a nice flavour. It should look gloriously clear; some years it looks clearer than others.

PICKLED WALNUTS

About 50 young green walnuts (pick mid-June)
Brine (To make, add 110 g (4 oz) to 2.25 litres (4 pints)
    cold water; make enough to cover your walnuts.)
2 litres (3½ pints) vinegar (whatever kind you fancy,
    cider is nice)
2 tablespoons black peppercorns
1 tablespoon allspice
About 3 tablespoons bruised ginger
A few bay leaves

You must pick the walnuts when they are young and green,
before the outer skin has started to harden. Prick each nut
several times with a needle. Wear rubber gloves for this –
walnuts weren't used as a dye for nothing. Place them in a bowl
and cover with brine.

Leave for a week, then drain and renew with a fresh brine
solution for a second week. Drain the walnuts, rinse and put
them on trays and leave them to dry in the fresh air. They will
start to turn black. This can take a couple of days. When they
are completely black and dry they are ready to pickle. Put the
walnuts into sterilized jars. In a large pot stir up all the vinegar
and spices, bring to the boil, simmer for about 10 minutes and
then pour it over the walnuts while hot, making sure they are
all covered. Seal and they will ready to eat in about a month.
They are apparently a peculiarly British delicacy, practically
unknown in Europe or the USA.

TOTALLY DELICIOUS RHUBARB TART
For 4 (or 2 greedies)

Pastry
Use a sweet, short one, and roll it very, very thin. The pastry is a vehicle for the filling. I don't care if you buy ready-made, although I make my own (smug moment); you can google the method.

Filling (the important bit)
First pull your rhubarb (about 3 sticks)
55 g (2 oz) light brown sugar
55 g (2 oz) caster sugar
1 large egg
1 tablespoon plain flour
55 ml (2 fl oz) double cream

Line a 21-centimetre (8¼-inch) pie plate with your pastry of choice; prick the base all over with a fork. Leave it to rest in the fridge while you prepare the batter. Cut the rhubarb into thin pieces and scatter over the pastry.

Mix the sugar and flour and then add the egg and cream. Whisk in a jug to make a light batter. Pour this over the rhubarb. Place the tart on a baking sheet and bake for about half an hour at 180°C (350°F) until it is just set and a pretty brown colour on the top. Serve warm.

6

Veg
in the Garden

T HERE IS ABSOLUTELY NOTHING NICER than fresh vegetables. This doesn't mean you have to go all kitchen garden, but just being able to pick a few beans or some salad leaves is a real treat. For one thing, when you are cooking really fresh vegetables (and I mean straight from soil to saucepan) they take no time at all to cook. You only have to dunk broad beans and, *voilà*, they are on the plate.

Nick has created the vegetable garden but no one could pretend that it is trouble-free. It is not the actual gardening time, it is time taken keeping the marauders at bay. I hate pigeons. What has a pigeon ever done for us? They love to give a good beaking to the base of broad beans, leaving the new shoots lying on the ground. They do the same with runners and French beans. Rabbits seem keen on leeks, but not onions and of course slugs just love anything leafy. It's not all bad news. Absolutely nobody likes rhubarb, courgettes, sorrel, potatoes (except eelworms,

which can bore through the roots), shallots, onions (except sometimes the onion shoots) or globe artichokes. Herbs are mostly a safe bet, but watch out for parsley. Everything else is up for grabs by someone.

I now have a decent salad bed but only because Nick thought to put in a netted raised bed, which was a game-changer. We now have brilliant chard and cavolo, which was unheard of before the netted area. In fact Nick has fantasies about netting the entire vegetable area. Snail and slug hunting is quite good sport, but wear rubber gloves.

I have learnt that it is absolutely *essential* to net the base of bean wigwams before you put in the seeds – just a small net about a foot high pegged down with a few metal pegs will do the job, otherwise they will be eaten before they've had a chance to romp out of harm's way.

Plant sorrel. You can't buy it in shops and it is a great, lemony addition to salads, and makes a yummy soup. It divides easily (just split is down the middle by whatever means you fancy and shove it in a new spot) and it will return year after year. You don't need much – a couple of large bunches. As soon as you see it start to go to seed chop it right down and in a few weeks new leaves will emerge. For some reason our local slugs don't seem to fancy it.

Globe artichokes are good for drama. We have two different types and as well as eating them they make a very exotic show or, as it is termed in the trade, 'architectural structure'. Cut them down when they look ropey. They won't make more heads but they will shoot back up again, making the area look fresher with their large silvery leaves. If you have got bored of eating them leave the heads to turn into wonderful mad thistles. I have planted an artichoke forest by a hedge just for fun.

Leeks are a miracle. The seeds are so tiny you can never imagine that they will result in anything at all. They go on for ever. Pull them as young leeks or leave them to thicken up. They don't mind what you do to them. Move them from one place to another if you want to free up space, they just don't care. The only boring bit about a leek is the thinning – taking out the surplus seedlings to leave space for one leek to get larger. Thinning in general is akin to vegetable torture: killing the fruits of your labour. Apart from potatoes, most vegetables planted from seed require thinning. This gives them the space they need to grow. Wait until they are large enough to handle and then start tweaking and chucking out the surplus until you are left with a nice space in between. To gauge this imagine the vegetable fully grown, and then add a generous couple of inches. It is absolutely no good thinking you won't bother. If you don't do it they won't grow to an edible size. You will soon get the idea.

Now structures . . . spend a bit of time making a proper bean wigwam, which is stable and not on the lean. Find long pea sticks and fix the netting on properly for the beans to cling to. If you are a bit Richard Rogers about the construction your life will be easier in the long run. Some years I have fudged the build, which has resulted in endless propping up and lots of extra work tying-in. You can use a good structure for a couple of years, so it is worth the effort.

Although our plot is small, we rotate the crops every year. That means not growing the same type of vegetable in the previous year's bed. This helps prevent disease and stops the soil from becoming depleted. Some vegetables also help the soil to improve. Just try to remember to keep things on the move (except the salad, you can leave that where it is).

Once you have started growing vegetables you won't be able to stop. Don't imagine you will ever be self-sufficient (you won't be), but the vegetables you do grow will give you more satisfaction than a cartload of supermarket produce. Don't get discouraged if one year a vegetable just doesn't take off. It can be for loads of different reasons – too much rain, not enough rain, eaten by pests, and so on. In the past I have attempted to grow things that were supposed to be simplicity itself only to find they didn't even have the courtesy to push up a leaf. Just relish the things that *have* grown and try out a couple of new varieties every year. Next time round I'm throwing caution to the wind and tackling flowering sprouts and the tree spinach 'Magenta Spreen'. Even with our plot we usually manage to find space for at least ten to fourteen different types of vegetables.

What we grow

POTATOES There are various types listed by the time of year when they are ready to rock. First early, second early, main crop – you get the idea. We usually grow three different types to ring the changes, but 'Pink Fir Apple' always goes in as it does very well in our soil. Nick lives in terror of eelworms and would have all the potatoes up before they have had time to develop. The wisdom is that they should go in mid-March and they can be dug up when the plants have flowered.

BEANS (RUNNER AND FRENCH) The more you pick the more they keep on producing. There are dwarf French beans too, but I like to see them rambling upwards.

BEETROOT A couple of rows

ONIONS AND SHALLOTS We do give space to these and l like plaiting them. Pull them when the leaves have wilted and let them dry out, either on the soil if the weather is good or on trays in the man shed. Drying out is key to preserving them.

BROAD BEANS The more the merrier. I usually put in a couple of packets.

CARROTS I am rather partial to buying seed tapes for carrots. It really does help when it comes to thinning. The seed is already spaced on a paper ribbon and you just lay it under the soil and lightly cover.

LEEKS Hooray for leeks. They always grow. Seed tapes are good for leeks too.

SORREL Keep chopping it back when it starts to seed, and it will start all over again.

BRUSSELS SPROUTS I only do about five plants, really just for Christmas lunch.

ARTICHOKES We seem to have room for about five.

SALAD LEAVES mixed

CHARD Just a row, keep on chopping it down and it keeps on growing.

SPINACH See above.

TOMATOES We only have about five plants but it is worth it, although the weather can be an issue, as they do like a bit of sun.

RIDGE CUCUMBERS Some years they do, some years they don't, but I still persevere.

COURGETTES About two plants (there are only so many courgettes I can face). Keep picking them as this is another plant that keeps on cropping.

FABULOUS VEGETABLE TIP

I have to give credit to Carol Klein from the BBC's *Gardeners' World* for the best carrot tip ever. Carrots are plagued by carrot fly and there are all sorts of tips on how to avoid this but I just *love* this one.

Plant your seeds in a large bucket and place it in a raised area. The Achilles heel for a carrot fly is height; even with good take-off conditions they are absolutely stuffed above 60 centimetres (2 feet). So while they are madly flapping around at the base you will be enjoying lovely carrots. This really works and I do it all the time now. In fact this year we upped our carrot game by replacing the bucket with the old bath when we upgraded. At first I told bemused passers-by we were turning it into a hot tub, but now Nick has clad it with boards from the old shed, so we are officially brilliant recyclers and have a tub load of carrots with good drainage through the plug hole.

SECOND HANDY VEGETABLE TIP

Buy a pack of mixed salad leaves (the kind you see in the salad section of supermarkets that are actually rooted and growing). Separate them into little plants and in no time at all you will have quite an advanced salad crop. This is miles cheaper than buying plugs in the garden centre, and I actually think cheaper than a packet of seeds.

SORREL SOUP

You can replace the sorrel with the tips of young nettles, which are delicious too.

Cut a large bunch of sorrel. Wash in salty water and strip out any large stalks.

Sauté a large onion in a pan with butter. Chop up a couple of potatoes and add them to the onion. Put in some stock (hopefully you will have boiled your own bones) and simmer until the potatoes have broken up. Add the sorrel. Keep on the hob until it has wilted (no time at all). Blend and serve with a swirl of cream, or even a sourdough crouton.

It is rather an unappetizing colour but I love the lemony taste.

7

Herbs
in the Garden

I F YOU CAN'T BE ASKED to go full-on with vegetables
then wave the flag for herbs. I cannot sing their praises
enough. Once you have grown your own you can afford to
behave recklessly in recipes, flinging in handfuls of loveliness.
Forget those stingy little plastic packets that hang in the
supermarket. A pot of mint soon turns into a bank and thyme
into a bush. Herbs won't let you down. They come back year
after year. They work in flower arrangements, food and are a
gift to the senses. Herbs don't care if they are in a window box,
pot or gravel. We are lucky – our soil is very well drained so
anything Mediterranean thrives. Herbs are not fans of very wet
conditions. I don't see how anyone could live without at least a
pot or two.

The absolutely must-haves

THYME

Thyme is hot holidays. Cut it back after flowering. Don't cut into the old wood or it won't sprout up again. It will go on for several years, by which time it may have become too leggy and you must start again. There are lots of different kinds of thyme, but *Thymus vulgaris* is common thyme and best for cooking.

I like to plant the flat carpet thymes in between paving stones so you can stamp on them and revel in the smell. Sometimes I cut a huge bunch, tie it with string and hang it up to dry in the kitchen. Then, when I need a thyme fix, I just pick it up and give it a shake and a squeeze over the pot. Mmmmmmmmmm.

MINT

Like you, mint travels. Plant it in the garden and it will pop up everywhere. Put it in a container to constrict the ranting. There are lots of different types – I love them all. Think of mint tea, mint sauce, chopped on to new potatoes, added to tabbouleh or, when it is getting too long, cut fronds for flower arrangements. Apart from plaiting it into rugs there is nothing you can't do with a bit of mint.

You will find some that has made its way round to the back door and can be located in the gravel path. This patch is really handy, as you don't have to go far – just stretch an arm round the door: from gravel to plate in an instant.

ROSEMARY

Rosemary is evergreen so you can use it fresh all year round. The leaves are oily and are rather nice if you tie a few sticks together and hang them under the bath tap for a free and easy bath treat.

Rosemary is covered with pretty blue flowers in the spring, and it is important to keep cutting it so it doesn't get too large and leggy. There are upright and trailing varieties. I just love the trailing *Rosmarinus officinalis* 'Prostratus'. It looks wonderful trailing over a wall or in a bed, its long fingers stretching out to make gorgeous ground cover. You will inherit several old rosemary bushes. They are too large really, but do we care? Just keep chopping. There is a very old bush by the back door (near to the mint). Even when the weather is challenging I don't need wellies to break off some twigs for the pot.

PARSLEY
Sow fresh parsley every year. You can divide and separate it, and sometimes it will carry on, but you will get better results by just sowing fresh seeds straight into a pot or the ground. If you forget just buy a pot from the supermarket and plant it on a nice day, giving it good soak before and after. It will soon double in size, thrilled to be let out of its plastic confines. I grow both the curly and the flat-leaf varieties, as there are definitely differences in flavour. The stalks are tasty too.

SAGE
You will always have too much sage. I only seem to use about ten leaves a year but they are a vital ten leaves. You can cut sage back as much as you like (and into old wood) and it springs back to life. Chop it back in the spring so it has time to regroup.

BAY
I use probably twenty leaves a year. The bay in the garden was bought as a tiny plant many years ago. It now takes a ladder and shears to contain it. It is easy to prune as the stems are soft. I have stripped the lower branches to reveal the shape (Bean's idea). Before it was a rather gigantic bushy shrub. Now, I am proud to say, it is a feature (Nick doesn't think so, but I love it). If you think it is too large, just go for it and hack it back.

BASIL

Sow basil in a pot from seed and you will get enough to make pesto for the whole season. I planted a whole bucket load this year, and Pigeon had every seedling. I hope he feels sick.

LOVAGE

You can't buy lovage in the supermarket so it really is worth growing your own. It comes back year-on-year and tastes like celery. It grows very high (about 2.5 metres or 8 feet), and is just the best chopped up in salads or added to soups. I think they make it into brandy in Romania, but that's one for you to try out.

CHIVES

Chives can be divided year after year. I have used them as a border 'hedge' around vegetable beds. It looked charming until it got entangled with the grass. Don't let them flower as then the soft stalks become thick, hard and inedible. Chop them to the ground, like grass and they will just grow up again. Start them off as seeds, or cheat and go to the supermarket and buy a pot. You can divide the herb into several smaller plants, which will soon double in size. When there is absolutely nothing to eat an omelette filled with chopped chives and mixed herbs is as near to heaven as it gets.

8

Mindfulness
in the Garden

B ACK IN THE DAY when the world was practising yoga I wasn't. Aura and chakra are just words to me, whereas you are up to speed on all the latest meditation techniques and regularly attend classes in this and that, so I am going to leave super-consciousness to you. However, if the idea behind the mindfulness movement is to be aware of the present and engage with your surroundings – then hooray, I am a grand master. Gardening is a completely absorbing activity. Many is the day I haven't fancied even opening the shed door, and after a winter indoors I can hardly bear to go outside, but as soon as the trowel is in my hand a weird mystical fog descends. It starts with a five-minute weed and ends two hours later during which time I have been totally transfixed. I may think 'that's a funny insect' or ' why are there so many stones when I took out five hundred last year?', but overall it is a quiet, totally peaceful occupation. Food and the need to pee being the only things that might drive me inside.

Vegetables are calming too. When they start to pop up in neat rows there is satisfaction that comes from being connected to the plot and growing food, even if the food is just a handful of holed leaves, and the broad beans just enough to fill a plate. Seeds are a constant source of surprise. Leave science aside and just look at a beetroot next to its seed to experience a mind leap into the unknown. When I sent for my wild flower mix, the leaflet that accompanied the packet advised me to take a pinch of seed, put it on to white paper and look at it under a magnifying glass so I could appreciate the diverse shapes in the mix. Only a gardener would think of including that on an instruction sheet.

Gardening is silent. The odd bird chirp maybe, or at worst next-door's strimmer, but not noisy noise. I don't want music or chat. Exercise soon expunges any irritations. Gardening is good for relationships; it's difficult to maintain a row when you need help shifting a huge stone or decimating a root.

On a perfect day, when the sun cast shadows through the hazel and there is golden glow over the field, all I want to do is stand and stare. Gardeners spend quite a lot of time looking; just call me 'Patience Clare' (well it takes months to grow an onion, and a full year to wait for a shrub to flower again). We talk about 'next year', but without any particular urgency. It's not wishing your life away, just preparing for the next cycle.

The only thing I don't do in the garden is close my eyes and breathe deeply (I do breathe, obviously) – and, well, I certainly don't chant either. I do talk to the odd weed, usually when I am trying to dislodge it from the earth and the conversation is basic.

Gardening dispels vanity. I can absolutely promise you that any need you ever had to take a selfie, or post a picture will be entirely overcome once you start gardening. The uniform is an absolutely hideous misshapen hat, any old jacket that comes to hand and various t-shirts and sweaters with holes. Hair is under permanent threat and nails a thing of the past. Sometimes I even shock myself at the end of a good gardening day. I absolutely get why it is tricky to look honed in the country.

Gardeners are on the whole very good at sharing. They really want to give you a plant, advise you on cuttings, donate produce and insist you take seed from their front garden. Obviously it might be daggers at dawn during judging at a giant vegetable show or waiting for a gold at Chelsea, but really sharing info is what gardeners do. Ask a question and you get a full-on answer, sometimes too full, but this will be very helpful when you are starting out.

So I hope you can see why I persist in the garden. It soothes the soul, and even I need a bit of that *de temps en temps*.

THOUGHT FOR THE DAY

'Ommmmmmm' said the little grasshopper.

9

Tooling Up
the Garden

UNLESS IT HAS BURNT DOWN (it is quite near the bonfire), you will inherit, along with the cottage, Nick's man shed. I am allowed to keep my tumble dryer in there, empty jam jars and a trug with my hand tools. Ted the dog is allowed to keep his cache of sardines and dog food in an empty cupboard. I am trying to sneak in extra stuff (outdoor cushions have found a corner), but really this is Nick's domain and he will have to leave you a list relating to the chisels, drill bits, nail boxes, files, choppers and metal tubes. Every item is an essential bit of kit for the hands-on homeowner. There is even a set of chimney brushes, which Nick uses to finish off the job once the sweep has departed. Our sweep is utterly charming and comes tooled up but sadly we found a couple of jackdaw nests left in place after one of his attempts at hoovering, and Nick really enjoys doing his Dick Van Dyke impression. The insurance company insist on an official sweep's certificate for their paperwork, clearly utterly meaningless.

There are some gardening tools that over the years I have found completely indispensable, and equally a few that are heading for eBay. The petrol-driven moss raker is a waste of space. We hadn't taken into account that the whole of our lawn is made up of moss with barely a touch of grass. So after an enthusiastic day's work with the new toy we were left with hard, uncompromising, bare earth – really hideous. The mountain of moss never broke down and I kept finding clods of it in the manure. We decided we haven't got the 'green line' lawn type of garden and the moss mower hasn't been used since. If eBay hasn't worked and it's still there, just leave it be, don't go on manoeuvres with it.

Out of all the power tools, the only one you really can't do without is a strimmer. If ours has given up the ghost then you will have to buy a new one. Buy a butch one (Stihl are excellent), as it has to cope with more rough than smooth. Never strim in the vegetable plot or the car park area if the car is in residence; the area is filled with flints. I found replacing car windows really boring . . .

You will see a spade with a long handle and a narrow red head. This is a fencing spade originally purchased for fencing. It is a brilliant tool. When you want to make a space for a new plant and the ground is hard and won't break up, bring it on. I use this spade all the time, you get a deeper hole than with a conventional spade, and I wouldn't be without it.

The rubber rake is another gardening essential. Use it on the flower beds to clear autumn leaves and it won't damage the plants underneath. It is brilliant on both gravel and grass and you will learn to love it, especially if the leaves are wet and stuck. You will use the other rakes too but this one is the only one for leaves, fallen fruit, etc.

In my trug you will find a metal tube with a handle on the top. This is a bulb planter. It really takes the effort out planting bulbs.

For a start you get the right size depth for planting and it also removes a neat plug of soil which you can drop back over the bulb. It makes the job much speedier and wins hands down over a bog-standard trowel. There are long-handled ones on the market too but I always use the short version and get down and dirty.

Nick adores his grubbing mattock. It has a pick handle with manly blades for trenching and earthing up. I think he just likes the word and loves to say ' I'll just get my mattock' in ringing tones. However, it does seem indispensable for clearing ground and removing large roots. There are mini mattocks and appropriately called roughneck mattocks. In mattock world there are men and there are boys.

There is a convex spade, which is for edging beds. Use this to shape the beds up, and get them back to size when they start growing over. It makes a good clean cut and is much better than an ordinary spade for doing a proper job.

Although it doesn't count as a tool, I am in love with the stone sink that Nick installed a year ago. One of a pair from lovely eBay; originally used for cattle salt licks apparently. Sink one is in a corner filled with rock plants and sink two, now complete with a tap and running water, is by the shed door. I use it for soaking plants, washing boots, cleaning tools (something I never did prior to the sink's arrival), and filling cans. It is a lovely thing. I am making it into a garden feature with old zinc watering cans and buckets positioned artistically around it. Nick has hung a brush on a long chain nearby so I can scrub away to my heart's content. Perfect joy.

We have bought a lot of spades and forks second-hand from local junk shops. Nick maintains they are much better quality than the new ones. He will be right on this one (indeed he could write the paper). They also have a look of use, and it is nice to imagine the DNA of previous gardeners on the handles (equally I can see this could put you off).

I am always throwing away trowels, forks and secateurs on the bonfire and compost. It happens when I clear up. I think everyone does this. I usually have a *déjà vu* moment a few hours later, hopefully before the handles have been reduced to charcoal.

It is easy to be seduced into buying tools but really you don't need that many. When it comes to anything with a blade buy the best, they are easier to sharpen and better to cut with. Bahco is our shear of choice and they do a lovely little pruning saw, another gadget I am most fond of. We have two types of shears for bed edges, one is for straight sides and cutting the overhanging grass and the other is flat and for cutting underneath shrubs and up to the beds. The topiary snail is trimmed with the kitchen scissors. Just call me Scissorhands.

The basic tool shed starter kit

HAND TOOLS trowel, small fork, secateurs (loads)
RUBBER BUCKETS
SPADE One to suit your size. I don't like using very heavy
   ones, they wear me out.
FORK as above
RAKE A rubber one and a metal one for levelling and sorting
   veg beds
HOE
BULB PLANTER
SMALL SAW
SHEARS
EDGING TOOL
STRIMMER
LAWN MOWER (obviously)
GLOVES You can never have enough; minimum requirements
   a thin pair and a robust pair for dealing with thorny issues.
KNEELING MAT A bit girly, but there are moments when
   you will be grateful.

If the shed does burn down buy the above and you should be able
to cover most gardening needs. A lopper could be good too, but
work your way up to that.

10

Trendy
in the Garden

WHERE TO START? I love a gardening trend. Even if you don't go full on, it makes you aware of ideas, different types of plants, and allows you to help the economy by buying lovely stuff like fire pits and pizza ovens. It also allows me to cogitate on plants I have absolutely forsworn and vowed never to give bed room to; whole groups of plants in fact. I told Bean to bury me now if I ever start to bring ornamental grasses into the garden. Yet recently I've found myself looking at them rather longingly, caressing the fronds and lingering near the stand at the garden centre. Bean is toying with pampas (a look we had definitely sneered at). Still, I absolutely draw the line at fuchsias and begonias. I love any type of dahlia but can't be asked to give houseroom to a chrysanthemum. Nick knows that buying me a bunch of flowers is a fraught experience.

I have always loved the 'inside outside' look, but this is trickier in a conventional cottage setting. We are working on a version by the garden table. Nick is in charge of this new project: drawing pizza ovens on the back of an envelope. We have taken a long time to get round to this on the basis that the number of times Nick and I think we will fall on a pizza is limited. However, now he has read that with the right amount of heat we could cook a turkey. That settles it. During a power cut it will have a major use as a second oven.

We don't light the garden, except with candles on a good evening, but if you do decide to go for it remember to light down rather than up. It is bad manners to inflict light pollution into other people's air space, especially in the country.

By the way while I think about it (and this has nothing to do with trends) why is everyone obsessed these day with shutting themselves away behind boarded fences? I have lost count of the number of local views that used to be shared and have now gone. Even small views count. A glimpse through a gate to the green beyond, gone, in the time it takes to replace a slatted gate with a solid one. Actually, of course, this *is* a trend albeit a horrid one.

We are putting our all into creating the ubiquitous wild flower area, but this is not proving particularly easy. At the moment of writing we seem to have a monoculture of ox-eye daisies. The first year it was a very pretty mix, and then it wasn't. I have had a long conversation with the wild flower maestro, who enquired if we had rabbits (ha!). Apparently they eat all the other small shoots but can't abide the ox-eye. He suggested we put rabbit wire round the plot and says he now does this on all his projects, which seems to rather defeat the object of a wild flower planting. I have now cut the daisies before they seeded and put a bit more variety into the bald patches, just what you shouldn't do, so we will see what comes about next year. Just so you know there are supposed to be about twenty different types of wild flower in the mix.

Cottage gardening always seems to remain in fashion. I don't think there is a year at Chelsea when you won't see one in the show gardens, holding its own among the vertical planting. Colours will change, and you may decide to go wild in the vegetable garden and grow an edamame rather than a runner, but a rose on an arch whether it's rusty, willow or stainless steel in a bucolic cottage setting is a classic.

I do wonder what trends you will go for? I have always rather longed to keep bees, and I am always envious of gardens that house quirky chickens. Maybe you will keep alpacas among the wild flowers – they could eat the ox-eye daisies or even trample the rabbits? You might change the garden furniture (but the wooden bench is an heirloom from my childhood so please allow it grass space). Corrugated iron, copper containers – ooh maybe a trickling Japanese water feature, rumbling over mossy stones . . . I haven't been allowed that *or* an outside shower (some rubbish about cost and pipe access).

One word of warning: beware trends in large and uncontrollable plants. The bane of my life is the leylandii hedge planted by granny when it was considered cutting edge in the sixties; and Japanese knotweed used to be thought a lovely addition before it started bringing down houses. Bamboo is also a tricky one, although I believe you can buy species that don't spread into the next county, and look where we are with rhododendrons.

Spanish bluebells are thugs – take them out if you see them. They are blue with bells but that is where the similarity to our native flower begins and ends. They are out to crush our wild drooping English bluebells, which are now under threat. You will know the Spanish boys, they are all thick, upright stalks and no scent. The Victorians introduced them as an on-trend garden plant and now they are running amok cross-breeding and encroaching into the woodlands, not near us at the moment but I am taking no prisoners. Despite my best efforts, a patch keeps reappearing on the border by the walnut tree, so I am relying on you to keep up the work.

Every year there are plants that have a moment in the sun and, like balsamic vinegar in my case, coconut oil in yours, you will wonder how you did without them. I am having a gaura fest at present; this is because I saw them looking wafty and fabulous planted in gravel in a small hotel in Portugal, and then they seemed to pop up everywhere I looked. I have planted a line in the Hendricks Walk. I am also very taken with salvias, which are appearing in the most beautiful jewel colours, and cheer up August. What trend will you spot and love? Please not begonias. If I see them going in I shall come back and haunt you – unless of course I've experienced a sea change.

11

Flower Pots
in the Garden

EVERYTHING ABOUT A TERRACOTTA POT is appealing: the colour, the shape, the texture and the variety of sizes. I have used one in the past to bake bread and the Greeks, when they weren't cracking plates, apparently chucked them with abandon into the sea during the festival of the garden of Adonis (I'm not sure why – to appease a tricky vegetation god I expect). Terracotta and the cottage go together. You could decide to go off piste but really nothing beats a piece of weather-beaten terracotta, the older the better as it will have taken on the elements. A bit of moss and ground-in dirt alongside a lichen make all the difference. They give a pot personality.

Pots are flexible. Shift them around. Dull areas become undull in the time it takes to lift and place. Mix and match, use different heights and shapes – they add variety to the garden and enable you to use plants which might otherwise have been rejected. If you fancy you can even pop a pot into a flower bed to fill an empty spot.

But here's the downside. Terracotta dries out really quickly. There is a notion that before planting up, you soak the pot in water overnight; this stops the clay wicking up moisture from the soil, depriving the plant. I don't do this, but it is an interesting idea. Terracotta pots aren't frost-proof, which means that in a hard winter they can crack up. The clay soaks up the winter water, which then freezes and expands, cracking the pot. If it is really cold you could move them to a sheltered spot, or even into the man shed. I have had a few breakages but nothing drastic. Keep the old pots to use as drainage crocks. You can buy pots that are labelled 'frost-proof', but it's not something I actively bother to seek out.

Choose plants that are robust. It's not an accident that pelargoniums are staple fare in a pot garden. Lavender, bay, helianthemums and that motorway favourite, the oleander, should all flourish; and, of course, herbs of any sort. Remember, you are expecting them to enjoy life in a constrained environment where they will run out of food and experience dry spells, so think about the plants you have seen suffering in the heat on holiday. If they can survive a summer on a roof in Rome the chances are they can brave a bit of drought in England. However, it is no use thinking you can just plant up and sit back. My heart bleeds when I see sad plants left to perish in dust on city windowsills. The more love and care you give your pot garden the longer the plants will last – hopefully years, with a few annuals bought in to satisfy a spending splurge at the garden centre. Deadheading and removing dead leaves cheers them up, as does adding a bit of soil to top up the pot every year. If you can be bothered they will enjoy a feed. Liquid tomato food is a good all-rounder, say once a month to keep them interested.

I am a big fan of an automatic watering system, especially when it comes to pots. They do need watering very regularly and plants are more likely to pass away through lack of water rather than too much. You will know when you are overwatering, the leaves start to go yellow and drop off. If you really overwater the roots will rot too. If you underwater the effects are also pretty instant. A two-week holiday for you, brown leaves and death for them. The soil should be moist, not compact. If you have used compost then never let it dry out completely or you will never manage to rehydrate it.

Nick introduced the automatic watering system. He loves the droppers, leaky hose, and mini sprinklers. His specialist shop of choice is hidden behind bike sheds and railway arches in south London. This is where after a hard morning's drive he can discuss the intricacies of the timer with other real men. All this information has been put to good use. Once set up, apart from remembering to change the battery once a year, all is a happy story. Each pot gets a couple of minutes dripping every day, which can be upped if there is a dry spell. They don't use up as much water as a sprinkler and so are also rather eco.

There is a movement that prefers a plastic bottle pierced with holes, filled with water and turned upside down in the earth, so it can slowly drip while you're away. Personally I would set my sat nav and go for the trickling droppers every time.

The golden rules of the pot garden

1. If you are planning to keep a plant from season to season there will come a time when it might need re-potting. Buy a pot a couple of inches larger than the one it has come out of.

   Turn the pot upside down, holding the plant so it doesn't tumble to the ground. Tap the base and sides of the old pot to loosen the soil; it should come clean out. Re-pot.

   If it is a very large pot, then you could just trowel out some of the old soil and replace with new. If the roots are touching the sides and it is really embedded, sometimes the only way is to break the pot but this is a bit draconian. Try cutting down the sides with a long knife first (don't panic about losing the odd fibrous root along the way).

2. Always put a good couple of inches of crocks/stones at the bottom of your pot to ensure good drainage. No plant likes its roots to sit in water.

3. Make sure there is a hole in the bottom of the pot. It sounds daft, but some I've seen come without, and drilling into terracotta is tricky (crack, crack).

4. Always water well after a re-pot. A good drink cheers us all up.

5. It is a good idea to put gravel on the top of the pot if you have some to hand. It helps to keep the soil moist as well as cool in summer and protected from frost in winter (and it looks pretty).

6. Bigger pots should have blocks underneath them so they don't sit flush to the ground or else they won't drain properly.

12

Chop, Chop
in the Garden

ARDENS GROW. This means you have to be a bit savvy about what, when and how to trim back. In some ways it is quite instinctive. If you are looking at a clumpy sort of perennial, say a hardy geranium, which has flowered and is now starting to look a bit of ropey then shearing all over is the way forward. Or if it has a single spike, like a hollyhock or a delphinium, cut down some of the flower heads and leave others to seed. By doing this you encourage more flowers and fresh leaves. Pulmonaria (lungwort), with their spotty leaves, can start to look very sad after flowering, but with a quick chop you will soon have a plant bristling with health and new growth.

You do have to know when to use a light hand and when to go for it as some plants don't like it if you cut into the old wood; best case they won't flower, worst case they will die. If you are having a panic attack about a particular plant, just phone a friend or google it.

Get into the habit of deadheading, you can't do enough, especially on the roses. 'Dies disgracefully' is a technical phrase used by the gardening fraternity (it applies to the plants rather than their owners, although the two could be symbiotic). It is when the old flower heads, rather than dropping their petals, hang on in a state of disarray, going mouldy. We have a few plants that come into the 'disgraceful' category, but they make up for it in other ways. The dianthus 'Mrs Sinkins' is an old-fashioned pink (who happens to be white), and is a classic example, but 'Mrs S.' smells wonderful, and I just pinch off the dead heads at the appropriate moment. The old rose on the front of the cottage is also a candidate, but it makes up for its shortcomings with colour and scent.

Talking of appropriate moments, in a burst of enthusiasm I once took all the flowering heads off the lilac, thinking it was over and had already flowered. I don't know what came over me. It was only when I looked down, surrounded by flowers, that I realized it was just thinking of coming out. Obviously I was trying to get on top of the gardening. Nick, although sympathetic at the moment of chaos, nestles this disaster to his chest and from time to time recalls the memory. It cheers him up to know I have feet of clay.

The first plants that I cut back after the winter are the epimediums. You will spot these from the bathroom window. They have pretty heart-shaped leaves and during the winter the top layer of leaves is always tinged black by the frost. Just shear off the old leaves and down near the base you will spot tiny flowers beginning to emerge. Go down as far as you dare, lose all the leaves, and then after a few weeks little yellow flowers will dance their way to the top. A week or two later new young leaves will grow to allow the plant to clump up. Timing is everything with this as you won't want to expose the leaves to a late frost, but if you leave it too late it will impossible to separate the leaves from the flowers and, although it won't matter to the plant, you will probably cut off the flowery treat. It is a bit of a gamble. There are a couple of different kinds in the garden, some with pink, others with yellow flowers, but they are trouble-free after their haircut.

Lavender is also quite specific. After the flowers have faded, just take off the stalks, and leave the rest. In the spring, around Easter, you can go for it. Don't cut into bare wood where there is no growth and stop where the plant still has spiky leaves, and all will be joy. Lavender can get woody and brittle, so pruning is important. It also makes the plants bush out to the side (a good look for lavender).

There is one shrub that you have my full permission to chop. The wisteria on the side of cottage was probably not the best idea, as the walls are short and it is long. The twining tendrils often find their way under the thatch and also through the bedroom window. This is absolutely *not allowed*. You can be as mean to it as you like and control is the key word . . . In February, when it is leafless, cut it to the shape and length you want. Cut back any new growth to a couple of buds, leaving a skeleton of a suitable size. In July or August, after it has flowered, cut back the whippy new growth, leaving just the stems you want to train. Wisteria is a thug. The one on the house next door in London rooted its way into the main sewer, causing £35,000 worth of damage. TFL had to close the red route. You have been warned.

When it comes to a shrub, it is a good idea to thin out old wood to encourage new. Your little saw (see page 46), will be good for this, or beefy secateurs. I love passing on this advice as I am hopeless at doing it myself. Although this year I have given various shrubs – philadelphus, cornus, viburnum – a bit of a hammering (and I must say they look all the better for it). I can now see through the shrubs, and have underplanted a bit. Reducing the height of the viburnum to reveal the philadelphus behind is a huge improvement. There was a lot of layer rooting in evidence and loads of old dead wood. I spent half the morning hidden from view under the bushes. When I had finished Nick remarked that it 'wasn't a good hair day', which went down well.

CUTS AND SNIPPETS

Hedges
It is against the law to cut hedges when birds are nesting (it also guarantees them a good night's sleep). So we usually have a go very early in March and then again in late August. We cut them down to chest height. This makes them miles easier to trim, and also gives us a view over the top. Sometimes over the years we have not been as determined as we should have been in reducing

the hedges and we live to regret it. Physically.

Always wear long sleeves when tackling the bloody leylandii. Not only does it grow ridiculously but when you touch the branches they produce a skin rash (double whammy). Don't cut into it too far or it will expose brown wood, which never recovers. Granny planted it, so blame her. I am actually now letting others do this hedge as I am not good at heights and balancing the ladder on the rockery is a bit scary. Nick doesn't mind the height but fusses that I am inclined to get bored holding the ladder.

Buddleia
Buddleia doesn't care what you do to it, which is why you see it sprouting out of buildings and on railway tracks. Butterflies really do love it (sometimes ours is absolutely covered). Cut the branches to a length that appeals and it will send forth a new branch. I cut it severely after flowering (you could cut it nearly to the ground and it wouldn't care), but if you forget tackle it in the spring. They just keep going no matter what. If you do manage to do it in it will be a first. Now there's a challenge for you.

Syringa
Try to deadhead the syringa (lilac) after it has flowered. It does help it produce flowers for the following year. If it gets too large, you can hack it back but it will then take a year off to recover, producing fewer flowers.

TOO MUCH OF A GOOD THING

Sometimes you don't want a plant to run riot, and then it is a good idea to cut off the seed heads before they get going. Alchemilla is a wonderful plant but it can get a bit too bold in a bed so snip off the flower heads before they seed. You won't remove them all but it helps prevent an explosion. Aquilegias and lynchis are both demons when it comes to reproducing so I take out quite a lot of the seedy stalks, leaving a few to do their thing. Valerian has fluffy seeds that waft in the wind and seem to have a 101 per cent success rate, so reducing them is a good idea too.

ROSES

Wear gloves and don't panic. Pruning roses really gets them going. Take out any dead wood and look out for suckers. You will recognize suckers, as they are always the healthiest and longest shoots in the pack and they don't conform; they might be paler or have less thorns. Cut them off at the base, you don't want them. Prune the climbing roses in the autumn so that long stems don't get caught up in high winds and break, and tie-in any loose stems while you're at it. With our roses, we mostly work on not having crossing branches. Cut out the spindly bits and try to open up the frame of the rose if it becomes too busy. We have several rugosa roses. They are brilliant where the soil is dry and poor – in front of the leylandii for example. They don't need much pruning but there is a startling white rugosa on the Hendricks Walk and it was in a very dire state, so I cut it back to the ground, and it has sprouted away, as though I had fed it the elixir of youth. Sometimes it really is kill or cure. March is a good time to start pruning the shrub roses; take them to about half their existing size, creating a nice even shape, and wait for them to shoot off.

You probably won't believe this, but pruning will soon become instinctive. Watch the roses and see how they grow, and prune accordingly. Just think shape and you won't go far wrong. The pretty rambler called 'Sander's White', which flourishes over the rusty arch, even gets attacked with the shears when it has flowered, I can't say it minds.

13

Brilliant Bulbs
in the Garden

B ULBS ARE FUNNY. They don't promise a lot when you put them in. If truth be told they are a bit of a leap of faith, but as long as you plant them the right way up (pointy bit upwards) they are the cheapest and most rewarding way to add cheer and colour to the garden. One thing you do have to get your head round is that you will certainly be planting them on a miserable day in October and a much more miserable day in November. It is at this moment the word sanity may spring to mind, but all good things come to those who wait and when they start to emerge in the spring you will be so thrilled your only thought will be 'I wish I'd planted more'.

Don't suffer a bout of depressive inertia when a vast box load arrives on the doorstep, planting won't take as long as you think. As long as you are equipped with the bulb planter (see page 44), it should be quite a speedy process. Don't plant in straight lines. Bulbs work best when you take a handful and toss them with abandon on to the ground, then just dig in where they fall. Vital if you want to create a natural drift in grass.

When planting small bulbs like crocus and snowdrops peel back a small section of turf with a trowel and tuck the bulbs underneath, placing the grassy cover back on top; they'll happily push their way through.

Most bulbs will reappear year after year, and will bulk up. Some will increase by seeding. The only ones you have to replace are tulips but I look on this as a good thing. There aren't many areas in gardening where you can up the colour scheme in such an easy and cost-effective way. I have to admit that I absolutely love a pre-chosen tulip collection. You will find these on all the websites. I am sure that this is considered by the gardening cognoscenti to be a total cop-out, but in the same way I like a clothes shop to give me a good edit, I appreciate a gardening catalogue that fires and inspires. I'll do the physical work and let them fret over the pairings. It's all too easy to get overwhelmed and end up just dumping the catalogue back on the pile. The only tulips you don't have to replace are 'species' or wild tulips, which naturalize by themselves. They will be well labelled in the catalogues and are little toughies coming back year after year.

I don't know which marketing team came up with the term (somewhere in Holland I expect), but all anyone talks about these days is 'bulb lasagne'. Heston probably has it on the menu already. It is all about layering bulbs in containers with a inch or two of soil where the béchamel would be. You then achieve a succession of flowers over weeks. I haven't done this yet but I like the idea of a triple-decker.

I have said this before (don't stop me if I repeat myself) but in case you glazed over that bit (see page 55), remember drainage in pots is very important, so put gravel or bits of old pots in the bottom of the container to prevent the hole at the bottom getting clogged. I have also put large pots on feet so they aren't flush to the ground. Otherwise in wet weather they can become stuck to the ground and won't drain, anathema for bulbs and roots. If you haven't got feet to hand, so to speak, use a couple of bits of wood. Don't block the hole!

Bulbs last for ages, the clever money is to choose some bulbs that flower early and some that flower later in the season so that you have a succession of loveliness. I am looking forward to planting acidantheras this year. They go in late and flower in August, just when most things in the garden are over, and they look glorious in containers too, so I can't wait. For the last few years BF Bean has been giving me a sack of narcissus every October for my birthday. They are all scented and make a delicious sight in the front garden by the bench. I have started to take a photo when they are out, so I remember where the gaps are. (This is a good idea for any garden area. You think you will remember what was where last year, but strangely you don't.)

Plant bulbs where they will give you the maximum impact from inside the house, when the weather is still cold/rainy/generally unattractive. Don't be mean – buy lots and then distribute them in smaller groups for panache. I now plant about sixty tulips in the long bed by the back windows, in groups of five to seven (always odd numbers). Plant them deeply and hopefully squirrels won't get to them. There are at least three different windows which look on to the tulips and when they are in bloom I do just stand and stare. The only really disappointing year was when pigeons and/or pheasants nipped off all the heads just when they were about to flower (actually disappointing is a slight understatement). Most of the time they give the bed a lift it doesn't have at any other time of the year, making it look (dare I say it?) really rather grand.

PLANTING TIMETABLE

The catalogues do the work for you on this as they sell bulbs in advance of the appropriate season, just like clothes.

Spring-flowering bulbs (daffodils, crocus, hyacinths, cyclamen, iris) plant by end of September/beginning October so they get to root up before it turns chilly.

Tulips November. Nasty bugs in the soil will have had their chips so the tulips are less likely to catch anything.

Summer-flowering bulbs (dahlia, gladioli, alliums, agapanthus) get planted in the spring when the soil is warming up; this prevents them rotting.

Stuff you should know about bulbs

Narcissus is the Latin botanical name for daffodil btw, in case you were getting confused.

Don't cut leaves off daffodils until they yellow (at least six weeks after flowering). Mow around them. You can pick off the deadheads to improve the look (in fact you must, otherwise the seed head takes all the strength from the bulb), but *leave the leaves*. This makes sure all the yummy goodness goes back into the bulb for next year.

Your bulb hole should be about three times the depth of the bulb you are planting. It is recommended to plant tulips as deep as you can so they don't get dug up. Sometimes the earth is too difficult, and I know I don't plant as deeply as I should. BF Bean told me that in a moment of desperation she once just chucked some earth on top and they popped up just the same.

Squirrels will get all your small bulbs, unless you cover them with chicken wire, which is not a good look in our small garden, so I can't be asked. I plant groups in different areas round the garden and hope they will miss a few . . .

All bulbs apart from crown imperials (*Fritillaria imperialis*) go upright. Crown imperials go on their side to prevent water going in the top end and rotting them. They are part of the lily family – large and showy. I have never done that well with them, but they are hotly recommended for cottage gardens and informal planting, so you may see them popping up. You won't miss them!

I love *Cyclamen hederifolium*. They really cheer up the garden in autumn. They always come as a bit of a surprise as they disappear below the ground in summer, and I forget all about them until the rather exotic flowers pop up hidden underneath another plant or in a patch of ivy. They look delicate but are pretty robust and are very useful for providing a pop of light under a shrub or shady tree. Clever gardeners seem to have them in bulk – I am working on it. Plant more.

Another unexpected autumn treat are autumn crocus.

They produce leaves in the spring, which then die back completely, but look in the front bed in the autumn and you will spot a group of delicate lilac flowers on long stalks. They like to bulk up and are a treat when everything else is on the wane. Greek slaves are known to have eaten them to make themselves sick, so try to keep Hendricks from stuffing them down. Symptoms are cramp, vomiting, increased blood pressure, weak pulse and death.

I haven't mentioned hyacinths. I particularly love them inside where they fill the cottage with scent. If you are going to pot up bulbs for inside then do remember that they will have to be held up by being kept in a cool, dark place for a few weeks, or the stalks will suddenly push on up, and then go on the lean before toppling over. Long twiggy branches provide useful support. Sometimes I use catkin twigs in the containers, which give the bulbs a bit of extra glamour, although they do drop a dusting of yellow on the tables.

14

Cheaply Does It
in the Garden

A N AWFUL LOT OF THE GARDEN has been produced on the cheap: dividing, seeding and layering from the existing plants. In the early days this was from necessity rather than a great desire to be a frugal gardener (as you know, shopping was invented to give me a hobby). This impecunious period resulted in a certain lack of planning, as I wedged in a bit here and a bit there; now I am trying to be a bit more selective but it will never be formal. I am not very good at formal in any area of life, so why should the garden be any different?

Gardens say a lot about an owner's personality. The other day a local village put on a garden open day. This is the sort of event that Bean and I relish, but she was otherwise occupied so it fell to Nick to fill the slot. He did terribly well, displaying a modicum of interest as we trailed the first five gardens, but then he took over the mini map and realized that there were seventeen gates still to be opened and fell into decline. I was sent ahead to yomp round while he sat moodily on various verges. WI cake and the promise of a Pimm's at number ten (sadly, the lady had gone inside at the vital moment) just kept him on the totter. Anyway, after doing the rounds there was one thought that stayed with me. It was very obvious who had help from outside designers, and who had created their own spaces. The designed gardens were perfectly nice, indeed smart, but they gave you no perception of the owner within. Until you own a stately home – in which case bring it on, Capability – do choose your own plants and create your own spaces. Who needs formulaic?

Some plants just multiply. Given the conditions in our patch you can't move without falling over pulmonaria (lungwort, it has the green and white spotted leaves, and blue flowers in spring), hellebores, lychnis and self-seeding myosotis (forget-me-nots). Primroses and foxgloves just love the dry chalk and the grass is littered with cowslips. Look out for the seedlings and start distributing them around the garden wherever you fancy, and then they will start to make a point in new areas. Erigeron, the pretty little daisy you had in pots on your wedding table, is popping up everywhere. It seeds in the smallest crack, and bulks up at an extraordinary rate. It has the capability to take over, so I am keeping a wary eye on its progress. There is a shocking pink hardy geranium that thinks it owns the rockery, while the soft, silver leaves of the prettily named lamb's ears (stachys) runs riot. The good thing about all of the above is they are easy to pull out and move around. With the number of pulmonarias I have discarded I could probably run a prosperous weekend sideline. The point is that you can divide loads of plants to fill in blank spaces.

I only have one statement plant. It came from granny's garden and is the giant tree peony, *Paeonia ludlowii*. I love everything about it. It has grown to be over 1.8 metres (6 feet) tall with the most beautifully wayward branches. It produces flat yellow flowers and the seed pods are fat and filled with huge black, glossy seeds. I tried to grow the peony from seed in the beginning and thought I had, lavishing love and care on the little pot for weeks, then granny turned up, took one look at the plant within and announced that I was nurturing a horribly healthy herb robert, a particularly prolific weed. I was very downcast, but to make up for my gloom granny waited until a seedling appeared in her garden and it was then transferred to mine, where it has flourished ever since. Perhaps you could have a go at hand-rearing, just to prove it can be done. This is a also a reminder that we all start from zero.

GARDENING FOR FREE

Take a cutting
I have taken cuttings from lots of plants. Some have done and some haven't. Mostly they have!

Softwood cuttings are the easiest to root. Take them in spring to give them the best chance (who wants to root at Christmas?). Cut a non-flowering piece of new growth about 10 centimetres (4 inches) long. Strip off all the lower leaves, and pinch out any growth at the top to minimize water loss. Fill a pot with compost, make a suitable hole (a chopstick is good for this), and pop in your cut stick. Firm in, water and label. Hormone rooting powder is recommended but it doesn't seem to me to make any difference. The label does. I had a cutting that didn't really flourish for years and then it took off. No idea what it was, and had to take it to the local guru for identification. It was a plumbago, obvious when she said it. Buddleia, lavatera, philadelphus are all examples of softwood shrubs. You will know when they have rooted as they will start producing leaves, and you can give them a little tug at the base to see if they are holding on. I have been known to just take them out and peer, but this is not recommended.

You can take lavender cuttings by the same method. Put several sticks together in the same pot. I have done a hedge this way, but it does take time to bulk up. I think lavender plants were more expensive in the olden days; they seem to be cheaper now. Lavender gets very leggy after a few years, but with a bit of advance planning you could have your cuttings ready to rock. Keep all your cuttings moist, don't let them dry out, and put them in a sheltered spot. Have a go with anything you fancy – what's the worst that can happen? Sometimes just leaving a cut stick in a glass of water works too, and then you can watch the roots appearing. I have had the branches in a couple of flower arrangements take off, but you do have to keep the sticks in water for a few weeks for a result.

Seeds
Obviously you can buy seeds but you can also gather them in autumn. Just nip off the seed heads when they are dry and put them in a *well-marked* envelope. Seeds come in all shapes and sizes. The walnut tree on the border was grown from a nut, helped on the path by squirrel, whose larder has now grown to bear many fruits for his family. When the foxgloves and the lychnis have ripened, I cut the stalks off and carry them carefully to a new spot before waving them madly to scatter their seedy goodness. I do start off most seeds in pots. It is always a moment of joy when they break ground, but it is sometimes a slow method of propagation. Some don't flower for a couple of years or more. I have taken seeds from my dierama ('angel's fishing rod' – yes, bought for the name), and plants are whizzing up, but I have read they don't flower from seed for five years, which even to me seems a long time to wait for gratification. Look out for self-sown seedlings too, and then move them around, giving them space to develop and grow.

LAYER ROOTING

This happens when shoots from the lower branches of a plant touch the earth and begin to send out roots, forming a new plant. Viburnum is good at this, as are philadelphus, cornus and syringa. I am always finding shrubs that have layer-rooted on their own – typically when I have been a bit backward in pruning. I just pull up a section and plant it elsewhere. I am trying to get the shrubs under control (I have allowed them too much freedom). Could I layer root you ask? *Yes!* Just bend a young supple stem so that it touches the earth, and loosen the soil underneath. Make a small cut in the middle of the stem and peg it down into the earth on either side of the cut (use a bit of wire or large stones). At this stage it is still attached to the main shrub. Firm down the earth, and wait. Check after about six months to see how the roots are getting on (gently, not violently in case they haven't grown on enough). When your new section has nice roots, separate it from the parent with secateurs and move to its intended location in spring or autumn when the weather is good for a transfer.

DIVISION

This is the simplest way to increase the plants in the garden. Don't do this in dry months (unless you are prepared to water, water, water, and then you could take the risk). Best to divide in the spring or autumn, but always water before and after you have divided, whatever the season. This is key. You can either dig up a whole plant and then cut it into sections using a fork or spade, or do it *in situ*, taking a new slice and leaving the rest of the plant behind. You must make sure that the new plant separates with good roots, a few leaves won't cut it. Once you've had a go and you see the divided plants thriving, your confidence will grow and no plant will be safe from your attentions. All the irises in the garden are from one plant. Just break off pieces of the tuber with a few roots on the bottom and place it in the ground. *Voilà*, a new iris (just lightly bury the roots, by the way, and keep the tubers exposed to the air – they like to feel the sun on their fronts). Any plants that look as though they are too clumpy will be ripe for division. The garden sedums, too, all come from division. In fact they positively relish it, the fleshy stalks are inclined to flop over if the plants get too large (you will see excellent examples of flopping in the front bed). Primroses can be divided easily, you can make loads of new plants from a clump just by gently teasing them apart. All the large oriental poppies, which are gloriously showy, are the result of a couple of moments with the spade.

Make sure you keep all the new plants damp for a few weeks after you've moved them. If the rain doesn't come, then give them a can. If they still look sad, sometimes I go for kill or cure, cutting them right back to remind them to grow. This often works.

15

Flower Arranging
in the Garden

Y OU REALLY CAN'T REPLICATE a vase of home-
grown flowers and leaves. Florists like to promise a
wayward bunch of cottage flowers but they are always
just too honed and it's not the same thing as going round with
the secateurs and filling your own containers. There is always
something to find when you start to look, even in August. You
don't need much of anything to make a display. Herbs are a gift:
sprays of rosemary, a couple of stems of lavender, mint that has
started to flower, they are all are a joy. In the winter months I
get a bit obsessed with denuded branches, especially the ones
covered with lichen. I love them if they are a several feet long or
just small twiglets in a tiny glass (visitors probably wonder why I
am harbouring dead sticks).

Flower arrangers love a trend. One year it's blackberries in
rusty tins, another year life wouldn't be complete without
a single stem of viburnum in a milk bottle. I saw a fantastic

indoor planting of beetroot last year; the red veined leaves were inspirational (you get the idea). It keeps a girl on her toes. Watch out for vases too, just like heels some are in today out tomorrow.

I once spent a brilliant day with Bean making *kokedama* (moss balls) from a YouTube video. We filled a table with our creations and felt gloriously smug with our mossy creations. Over the years terrariums have resurfaced a couple of times, but in slightly rejigged formats, and it always pays to watch out for trends in house plants. By the by, never ever buy a weeping fig – the *Ficus benjamina* tree – whoever gives them the thumbs up. They look a treat in the shop but all the leaves seem to drop off on the way to the car. Be warned. I have seen some rather jolly plastic ones.

I am having a 'furious with florists' week. They all construct delicious bouquets that are vase-ready, but they don't bother to condition the stems, which means they are guaranteed to flop over and die after a couple of days. If you don't condition flowers before they go into water, the chances are very strong that the water won't go up the stem and they will wilt pretty speedily. This irritation applies both to florists who should know better, and smart market stalls where the staff can tie a sensational bunch with one hand behind their back, but couldn't care less how long the product lasts. Once a bouquet has been tied it is quite hard to start breaking down the stalks. Many is the display I have seen languishing at a bedside through simple lack of care.

Conditioning just means prepping the stems of the cut flowers or leaves. If you do just a tiny bit of work, they will last for ages. There are tomes written on this subject, but I have got it down to a few must-dos. A floristry school might think otherwise.

The Clare Hastings 'it works for me' conditioning method

I always add a quarter of a Milton sterilizing tab to the vase
water to keep it clean and fresh. Nothing is nastier than
murky, smelly, flower water. Milton is just as good as all
those tubes of flower food you get. Remember to top up vase
water. As with people, some flowers drink more than others.

Strip any leaves from the stem that will go into the water or they
will rot.

Re-cut all the stems, take about 5 centimetres (2 inches) off the
bottom if you want to keep the length, or cut to suit.

I use a small hammer and a chopping board to break up the
bottom of woody stems (roses, leafy stems, stems from
shrubs). I believe this is frowned upon (bacteria fest) and
cutting up the stem is the preferred method, but heigh-ho.

Boil some water and put it in a jug and then plunge the bottom
5 centimetres (2 inches) of flower stalks in for about twenty
seconds. This stops drooping, which is caused by air locks
in the stems. It seems harsh but it works with pretty much
everything.

It is recommended that you put cut flowers into water for several
hours before arranging them but I never have the time, and
just do the above, which works for me. If you are picking
round the garden then do cart round a bucket of water and
stuff them straight in. This is working on the theory that
they won't know they've been picked.

Just one other thing . . . You may notice tiny black insects
emerging from your cut flowers. These are pollen beetles
and they do what it says on the tin, feed on pollen. Sweet
peas and marguerites are particularly prone. Just put the
cut flowers for about five minutes in the bath (minus water).

The pollen beetles will be attracted to the white enamel and just totter off and then you can hose them away. Tapping the bunch (lightly) against the sink works too, as would a sheet of white paper. If you leave them on the flowers they are inclined to be found days later frolicking over the windowpanes. They are longing to go into the light.

16

Tweeting
in the Garden

I HAVE BECOME something of an expert on blue tits. I'm not saying it would be my specialist subject but I could probably handle a short guest slot on *Springwatch*. The first time I really ever gave a blue tit more that a cursory glance on the bird table was a few years ago. I was looking out of the window when I noticed two small birds engaged in what I assumed was mating. After a few more seconds the birds were looking a bit less Mills and Boon and more *Fifty Shades of Grey*. I realized that I was witnessing a fight to the death. One of the blue tits was dive-bombing the other, over and over again, aiming for the centre of the head. Indeed blue tit two was quite bloodied. I nipped outside. Blue tit two was a sad sight. I took him to a sheltered spot in the garden, where of course I should have done a dignitas, but weedily I left him looking peaky and hoped he would mend. I have been looking at blue tits slightly more analytically ever since. Then a couple of Christmases ago I gave Nick a bird box with a camera inside. I had been thinking

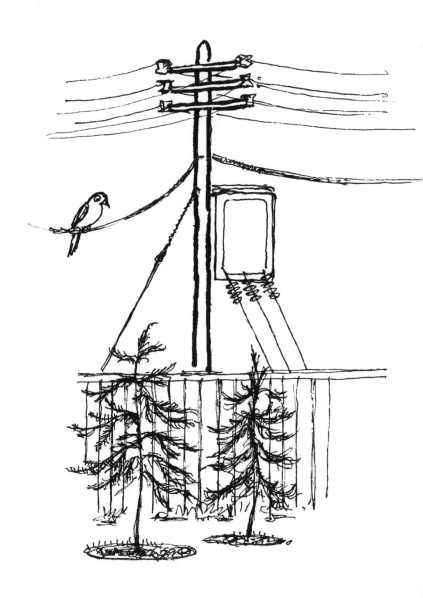

of getting one for some time but they are pricey and I was feeling mean. Anyway, now I wish I had bought one years ago. Forget a box set, a bird box is the way forward.

I never really thought a bird would actually use it, but we do have a lot of blue tits and the box was designed with the right-size opening to appeal to a first time tit owner.

Year one, result! Billy and Beryl blue tit took up nesting rights. Here are ten things you never knew about blue tits.

1. They are really fussy nest builders. If the interior isn't up to the mark they take out literally every piece of moss and straw and start again. They pick and twitch at one bit until it is exactly to their taste.
2. They lay loads of eggs. First year, ten (that is a lot of chicks to a room).
3. When they start to hatch Beryl blue tit goes on the vertical in her efforts to shift eggs and chicks around so they all get their share of warmth and food and don't get squashed. She never stops arranging the team. She is quite the athlete.
4. When asleep she fluffs up like a round tennis ball. She is in by sunset. Billy can stay inside until she has started to lay, then he is back outside in the hedge.
5. When the chicks start to move about, they turn themselves bums up and poop out what appears on camera to be a small white crisp. Beryl takes this in her beak and removes it from the nest. Very impressive sanitation levels.
6. Billy is allowed to help with the feeding.
7. The chicks are absolutely adorable until they start to fledge and then they turn into the teenagers from hell. Poor Billy and Beryl have to run the gauntlet of hideous open beaks, and what amounts to a gang mugging as they attempt to feed the brood. I have to look away.
8. When they start to fledge they use each other as a tower and

the strongest flaps his way to the top of the tower from where he (or she) can launch himself out. The ones at the bottom can get trampled to death. They were the weakest and probably the last to hatch.

9. Each couple has very different characteristics. Last year's were joined at the wing and spent three weeks roosting side by side before even attempting to redecorate. Others clearly met on Tinder.

10. Blue tits have endearing qualities, but overall turn off the camera before the fledglings get too large and then the violence is just too much to bear.

Clean out the box every September. This isn't a major undertaking; just take out the old nest and brush out the odd bone or two. The nest is much taller than it looks on camera, about 15 centimetres (6 inches) and of course square. They like it clean in case they need to shelter over a hard winter, and new couples like a fresh box in spring. Start to check the box from mid- to late March for the first signs of activity.

Of course we have constant arrivals from other birds. Rooks can cause a stir en route to the rookery. Sometimes you look out and it really is just like the Hitchcock film. Hundreds are lined up on the telephone wire or clinging to the leafless tree branches. They are extraordinary and sinister. Then suddenly, just when you feel attack is imminent, they all take off back home.

The red kite, which was a threatened species, has made too good a recovery since it was introduced back into our area about eighteen years ago. I counted twenty-four wheeling their way over the village the other day. They are protected (not for long, I should think). They are huge but can often be seen being put upon by crows, who will see off anybody.

Our ancient bird table planted in the front bed is one of my favourite possessions. It is only a couple of feet from the kitchen table and provides the ideal spot for the lazy twitcher. We can all eat together. Nick says I am baiting in the rats but I know the rats will come regardless. I stopped feeding the birds for a whole year as a control experiment and it made no difference to the rat count at all. I don't feed during the spring and summer, when they are supposed to forage for themselves. Interestingly, while Bean's London birds eat anything and everything, our cottage birds wouldn't touch a piece of bread if Mary Berry herself had breathed on it. I made them a special 'cake' one year with fat and seeds. They hated it.

A word of warning: beware the arrival of the fieldfares. They flap over from Scandinavia and favour a berry. They move in a pack and our holly tree can be stripped of all the berries over a weekend (meaning none for Christmas). Pick some holly first week of November and put it in a bucket of water in the man shed. It will last through to Christmas. Granny would have me pick it in October but this is extreme (all the odder as she was no fan of Christmas).

We have several old bird books, so Hendricks can spot and tick. Some have made the descriptions so complicated that identifying anything other than a pigeon is a Mensa exercise, but there is one faded one that came from a service station shop and it has a proper photograph on each page which makes it a winner for me. I read the other day that fish have regional accents; I wonder if birds do too? If so it would make the fieldfare chatter most entertaining. I shall look into it.

17

Wallpapering
in the Garden

THE COTTAGE ISN'T CALLED 'Bankside' for nothing. Everything is on the slope. Before Nick embarked on a floor levelling exercise in the hall, wine glasses would slide down the dining table in an entertaining way, literally breaking the ice at the party. The low wall at the back of the cottage was one of the first building projects – pre-wall the earth sloped down into the back of the house making damp patches on the walls. The gravel path round the house now acts as a soakaway for the rain and the retaining wall has made one of my favourite beds in the garden. It means I can garden like an old person without having to stoop, and I can pick out weeds as I go past. We don't have walls anywhere else. Granny was mean about our wall – too many bricks, apparently. In fact she made us so nervous that we stopped a course short on the second pillar where the steps are. That's why they aren't symmetrical. It looked daft, but an ivy that Nick bought as a house plant somewhere back in the day, and which became part of his divorce settlement, took root and now covers both the steps and the pillars so you wouldn't guess we are a brick or two missing. If you ever decide to take the ivy away you will notice (maybe you could still add another tier). By the way, give the ivy a hard clip back a couple of times a year to keep it neat and contained, otherwise you won't see the steps or the wall.

After the 'too many bricks' comment, we were keen to start concealing their bricky loveliness as speedily as possible and, as luck would have it, trailing plants are some of the simplest and most rewarding plants in the garden. Some start off as small plugs but by the end of the season have bulked up at an extraordinary rate. I replace some from time to time but with a bit of judicial clipping they should last for many years. The wall itself has weathered splendidly. The top edge is covered with a layer of fine moss, and wild strawberries have crept into the crevices. Some years a foxglove manages to seed itself on the top and miraculously clings on in despite the lack of soil, albeit at a languid angle.

WHAT'S FALLING OVER THE WALL?

I love *Iberis sempervirens*, or candytuft. It is a good idea to have a couple of evergreen trailers so you don't get winter brick exposure. Candytuft is very tidy and you can cut it right back to keep it in shape. In the spring it is covered with the whitest of white flowers – they glow. It is absolutely reliable and I think there are four now (one sneakily layer-rooted on its own).

The little daisy *Erigeron karvinskianus*, which came from your wedding table, is officially everywhere. It seeds like a weed but is very controllable. Just pull it out if it turns up in the wrong spot. It has the longest flowering season, and if you see it going to seed just cut it back and it will start up again. You can take it right back to the ground and it will just get going again . . . It is a lovely cottage plant and falls over the wall in the gentlest way.

I am a huge fan of helianthemums (rock roses). Buy them as small plugs around Easter time; they bulk up at a remarkable rate – practically as you look at them. The single flowers are the prettiest and they keep on flowering, on and on. When you think they are over, clip them back to just before the old wood and see them start up again. After a few years, despite the clipping, they become a bit too stalky so just buy a couple more. They come in loads of different colours. I, of course, seem to gravitate towards the pink and white ones.

In the corner you will note a lovely daisy with silver leaves, *Anthemis cupaniana*. It spreads at a thumping rate. If it gets too large, ruthlessly pull it up. Sometimes I think it is looking too bulky and I take it all up, leaving just a few pieces which I push back in and off it goes again. I take off the dead heads so it will carry on flowering, sometimes right through to November. It hangs over the wall in a very pleasing fashion.

Next door is a hummock of cerastium (snow-in-summer). It also has an irrepressible nature and is another plant I have to pull up by the handful to stop it taking over. It's all in the name – it gets covered with white flowers in early summer.

Every cottage garden should have a couple of aubrietas and so I do. At the end of the season lift each plant up and check underneath. Often it has died off, so I cut away all the dead rubbish to give it a bit of pep for the following year.

Centre stage is the hardy geranium 'Johnson's Blue'. It is a favourite, and more usually found as a ground cover plant, but it forms a neat clump and loves the position. It continues flowering from May through to August. Gardeners get used to watching the weather. I always know that there will be a week of violent winds just when 'JB' is in its prime. The wind causes it to split and fall over, covering the top of the wall. The wind comes as no surprise to me, although it always seems to cause a sharp intake of breath at the Met office (as does snow in early April, which is a regular occurrence round our way).

I hope you will love the wall. The plants that paper it are very giving and meld into each other in a very promising way. It is the only bed I feel I have some control over, I am sure it has to do with the height. Keep the plants low so that you get a vista to the shrubs beyond (that was my intention). I planted a spiraea outside the bathroom window and it has grown much too large. I cut it back severely after flowering but it has outgrown the spot and I definitely bought the wrong one. There are loads of different types, and that one has an excess of growth hormone. I may change it but I have a problem replacing shrubs that insist on flourishing.

18

Forever on the Weed
in the Garden

WEEDS ARE BY AND LARGE UNDESIRABLE. Some must be resisted at all costs, others you learn to live with. Be on a constant lookout as you dig round the garden, there will be some splendid examples for you to study. Never think you just pull up a weed without an implement. The leaves will come away in your hand leaving behind the roots, which will live on and thrive. Unlike the plants you want to grow, which can be a bit hit and miss, weeds are horribly robust and some would carry on even if you gave them a bucket of bleach and went at them with a flame-thrower.

The laughably named 'lawn' areas in the garden are weed infested. We long ago gave up trying to make them anything other than cottage grass. If you want a proper lawn a lot of work is required to aerate the soil and then weed and feed, so I don't. Everything from plantains to daisies is allowed to grow in the grass. Although I do draw the line at thistles, as they are prickly and I like to trip about barefoot when the sun shines, so I concentrate on just this one type of weed and let the mower shred the rest.

There are woody weeds, flowery weeds and also the tree type. Keep a watchful eye out for sycamore seedlings. We are surrounded by the trees and their terribly efficient twirly seed. At least three were self-sown and if the garden was left untended for a few years, we would revert to being woodland in no time at all. If they manage to push out more than just a few leaves from seed they are tricky to get out. The taproot heads straight on down and, after a certain point, it takes quite a lot of digging to remove it. I sometimes see them taking root in other gardens and want to immediately shout 'danger, tree alert!' The poor unsuspecting souls have no idea what is about to dominate their garden and the amount of leaves they will drop. Don't get me started, but raking them up certainly concentrates the mind.

Squirrel helps spread walnut trees by digging in the nuts for his winter store. Our walnut tree is from one of Squirrel's nuts and I can't believe how vast it has become. An avenue would be very nice but we haven't the room. Every year when I'm planting bulbs I come across a cache of walnuts here and there, along with hazel nuts (don't let them get going either; a hazel coppice is all very well but that grows apace too).

Some plants start off with the best intentions and then you suddenly realize that they have taken over and are suffocating everything else. Ivy falls into this group. It can get into the crown of a shrub and before you know it you have an ivy bush. Equally when you look up, suddenly there's a tree infested with the stuff; it weakens the branches and stops the light. Try pulling away at the stems whenever you see it, or cut the larger roots off at the base to prevent its growth. The only place I am actively encouraging it to grow upwards is the electricity pole, a very unlovely feature which the board surprisingly erected when we away on holiday one year. Ivy also has a place under the leylandii, where it covers the tricky bank and helps to hold in the soil. It doesn't root too deeply and you can inflict quite a lot of damage if you go for it, but having said that it is very, very determined, and you can't take your eye off the stuff for a second.

Nettles are shallow-rooted too and as long as you wear gloves, you can pull them out fairly easily, but if you leave one little bit of root behind (and you will) then the nettles will pop back up. Bindweed falls into this category too. Leave a tiny bit of chopped root in the soil and up grows another, and another and another. I pull them up whenever I see them twisting their way on. If you leave them to grow up they will drag the plant down. I could mention ground elder but I think that I may be in danger of depressing you, so I'll leave you to find out about that on your own.

It's odd how some jobs just don't appeal. I can't bear filling up the car and emptying the dishwasher is terminally dull. The garden task that has me glazing over is watering the gravel with weedkiller. I would much prefer to root out the weeds by hand than open a packet, work out the quantity of water needed, find a stick for swirling the water and then walk up and down sprinkling the mix over the path. I don't know why this is. The stuff works so you would think it would be quite a soothing occupation but more theatre would help the process along – I would like to see the weeds actively shrivel before my eyes. We were advised to glyphosate the wild flower area before seeding – basically getting rid of one lot of weeds to replace them with another, which seemed a bit ridiculous at the time. Treat glyphosate with care, your beloved godfather decided to drench himself in the stuff using an industrial spraying system which came with a backpack. He ended up with the most enormous spongy swelling on his shoulder as a result. It went down with seemingly no dire effects, but it was a reminder that it *is* a deadly poison. While I think of it, ragwort, which is a very common wild flower/weed and is tall with bright yellow flowers, is also toxic to horses and cattle. Nick pulled out a large plant the other day without gloves and his arm and hand came up in red weals, which lasted ages. Keep James on the strimmer, this keeps the nettles down to sensible level and gives the garden a veneer of polish. Insist on glasses or goggles for him and keep your distance. You would be amazed at how far a small stone travels.

A beginner's guide to weeds you will have to tackle regularly

BRAMBLES A woody weed, it sends down suckers and is very invasive if you allow it to take hold.

THISTLES Quite easy to remove, wear gloves.

DOCKS They have a deep tap root and so dig out carefully.

DANDELIONS Get them out before the clocks start to spread seed in the wind.

BUTTERCUPS Creep and spread in no time.

HERB ROBERT All over the Hendricks Walk, but easy to pull out,

RAGWORT Favours the roadside bank. Also easy to pull out, but toxic, so wear gloves.

GROUND ELDER Don't ask. Learn to live with areas of it.

STINGING NETTLES Their roots run for quite a long way and it is important to ease out *all* the root. You could spray them but I usually dig out as much as I can. The leaves can be mixed with water to make fertilizer.

BINDWEED You will never get it all out but pull out the tendrils from the base before they start to use your plants as stakes and twirl upwards.

IVY Pull it out regularly when you see it aiming for the flower beds.

MOSS Moss is just moss . . . I don't think it is a weed as such but it is *everywhere*. We are officially a moss garden. Try to take it off the base of plants when you see it taking over. The only place I really like moss is indoors, with bulbs. I used to think it was pretty, now I know better.

Try to tackle the bigger weeds early in the year when the ground is still soft and they are still small. Leave it too long and in our dry garden removing them becomes a bit of a saga.

19

A-Musings
in the Garden

GRANNY AND A POSSE OF HER FRIENDS used to have a mantra that was repeated every time one or other of them rang to arrange 'drinks'. After the date and time had been set, before signing off, they would to a man repeat the sentence: 'Now don't forget dear, you really must come early and see the garden.' This is a sentence I haven't heard since. Does a garden need to be a certain size before you're required to 'come early'? The cottage garden would be a very quick tour. Most of my friends wouldn't know if I had raised a rare plant or if it was a dangerous weed. If I asked them to sample different botanical gins in the garden I think they could probably be relied on for an early turn up but of course I simply couldn't guarantee that the overall appearance of the garden would be worth seeing. Maybe if it was a very last minute, spur of the moment sort of drink, and it was June with the sun was shining I could tentatively enquire if they might like to glance round. The fact is that as soon as it was completed there was a

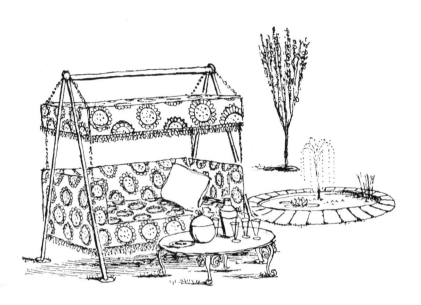

queue to look inside the new man shed, but I can't remember anyone saying 'Oh, do let's take in the rockery.' I might reintroduce the concept of a walk round and gauge reactions.

All gardeners love the National Gardens Scheme. The Scheme raises money by asking individuals to open up their gardens and donate the visitor proceeds to charity. I have seen some really lovely gardens, and it is a treat to be allowed to poke around different plots, getting ideas and inspiration from gardens of the great to the 'just good' gardens. However I am equally pleased to visit someone who has a garden and absolutely zero interest in cultivating it. Preferably it should be weed-filled, with the lawn needing a scythe. It really cheers me up. I know this is a bit perverse but it means that when I get home, instead of moodily looking around wondering how I can improve things, I start to think 'it's not so bad really'. Maybe there could be a tour of really hopeless gardens. I think it would be a tonic. I'd go.

Ha, ha! Nick spent an hour last weekend trying to fathom out what was off kilter with my autumn flower arrangement. I caught him standing just in front of it, mesmerized by sprays of blackberries. 'I thought the blackberries were over,' he mused. Half an hour later back he came. 'What are those twigs? Have you put something on them?' Another half an hour passed and clearly unsettled he started to prod them. More interrogation followed, until the forced confession. '*Yes* they are plastic! I love them. Do they look real or what?' I remember at school we were sent off to visit and give good cheer to the local old folk to improve our social awareness skills. I used to go once a week and talk to Miss Scott, who favoured manhandling tea bags before throwing them away ('remember to give them a good squeeze dear') and just loved the plastic daffs which came free with the washing powder. Fired and inspired, granny decided she would also do her bit for Miss Scott and ordered up a plastic arrangement of exquisite beauty, all trailing ivy and leaves. Miss Scott took one look and sent it back; too real! Well, I have added real garden sticks to mine, and far from returning my plastic I am cogitating starting up a large and rare collection.

I completely get the obsessive nature of a detectorist. One of the pleasures of digging in our garden is keeping on the lookout for what lies beneath. Both the cottage and the vegetable plot have yielded treasures and, just when you think there is nothing else to discover, up pops another treat. We have loads of small glass bottles, which give a history of domestic events in the cottage. Bottles containing permanent wave lotion, medicine and beer bottles, bottles marked 'poison', bottles with glass stoppers and a couple with marbles inside (used to keep the fizz fizzing). I found one recently with 'Made in Reading' written on the side along with company letters and a number. When googled it turned out to be from a glass works which had supplied breweries all over the country.

The factory closed its doors in 1913, due apparently to the arrival of cheap Swedish imports.

Nick turned up a rusted heavy ball in the vegetable plot, which after investigation turned out to be a grenade, *circa* 1644, most likely mislaid on the way to the Battle of Newbury in the English Civil War. We found a charming eighteenth-century china pipe tamper in the shape of a gartered leg, lying under a patch of weeds. It was all in one piece, which was a miracle, as goodness knows how many times the plot had been dug or mowed. While rotovating the vegetable bed Nick also spotted a tiny *blanc de chine* porcelain figure of Christ on the Cross; this was broken at the base so we are madly looking out for the bottom half. Less interesting but still emotive are the horse and donkey shoes that turn up, and the little pieces of broken china from all the mugs, cups and teapots that found their way to the various rubbish dumps positioned round the borders. I rather like an old die-cast blue toy car that appeared. We have a couple of buttons and some pennies. I keep it all. Treasure. Lives lived.

Nick does not relish travel. He likes it once he has reached his destination but the process of moving from A to B sends him into dark places at least two weeks before we are even *thinking* of leaving. Every time I mention the forbidden word 'holiday' or start waving travel articles in his direction I get the same response 'Why can't we just look at the photographs?' Well, this is all very well and good, but the point of travelling is not the large picture but the small details that never crop up in a brochure. This particularly applies to plants and plantings. How else would I have discovered that the best way to grow and crop strawberries when space is limited is in a length of galvanized guttering, which we spotted one evening attached to the roof of a taverna in Paxos. I never knew you could grow a bulb without soil or water, until I bought a giant colchicum from the Tulip Museum in Amsterdam, and one look at the blocks of gaura wafting in a Cape Town garden transformed the way I thought of planting it. Thank you Pensão Agricola in Portugal, where we ate outside to the scent of herbs planted in a plastered wall set at table height. In a languid moment between courses you could brush the leaves releasing the aromatic smells into the air.

Every cutting brought home and successfully grown on is a major triumph and a living reminder of holiday happiness. So the bleats of complaint fall on absolutely deaf ears. I put his passport into my bag (Nick will try every trick to avoid the airport – you will remember when he left his front tooth behind), and shovel him along.

Of course he really couldn't bear to miss out and was online ordering the guttering before we'd left the island.

20

I Wish
in the Garden

IF I HAD THREE WISHES from the genie and the lamp what would I wish for? I am going to really think about this. I know what I don't wish for – a swimming pool. I have seen too many languishing covered and unloved during a dubious summer and a hot tub is not very cool (only good if you live in a Scandi country and favour a dash through the snow for a hot bubble). Natural ponds are beautiful but I don't think of myself as a wild water swimmer (what lurks beneath?). The British and water always make a tricky combo. I really *did* want my outdoor shower but probably not enough to lavish a wish on, and the truth is I am only feet away from the one indoors. All the same . . . boo hoo.

I don't want anyone else's garden. I don't get garden envy very often and even when I do, I wouldn't want to actually move. I have been here too long; it is in my bones. I know that some love the stimulation of change. I love the stimulation of moving the familiar forward, remembering how it was, and how it has become. It gives me a sense of achievement, although, looking around, the achievements aren't by the standards of *Grand Designs* very large.

When I first moved into the cottage there wasn't a garden, just long grass and the patch of rhubarb, and so it stayed for a couple of years and then it started quietly to develop. Areas that were wild have been taken in and now we manage some kind of disorganized care in every area, including the triangle of land across the road, which was a hazel copse and filled with old dead stumps and rubbish. After looking at it for years, Nick got the bit between his teeth, and persuaded various village friends who owned butch machinery to help in root removal. It's now the vegetable area. 'That won't work,' said a particularly laconic local. Ha, ha, it did. To say that we are slow movers would be an understatement but I am trying to pick up the pace.

I wish I had a bit more time. Friends for the weekend, or even just for dinner, are tricky. It puts gardening absolutely on the back shelf. It is no point even pretending to attempt anything. Holidays are difficult to plan too. The only time I am absolutely happy to leave the garden is January; all the other months are taken up with some sort of soil shifting or another.

I used not to mind missing the grand opening of some flower or other, now I find I do mind. There is no doubt life gets in the way of gardening. Sometimes when we have dispensed with life and just done the garden, you really can see quite a lot of progress. A longer week would be a good wish.

I'd like to get a proper grasp of borders. I am best at just stuffing things in rather haphazardly. Fundamentally I feel uneasy with this. I think I would like some sort of chart system with nice drawings, although I probably wouldn't be able to stick with it.

I am too easily distracted by plants, buying on impulse without thinking about a proper scheme. I'm more of the 'ooh, there's a space there' sort of a gardener. I have been worrying recently about the gardening heart-throb Monty Don. His garden on the telly is starting to look rather crowded. He is now beating a path round jungle terrain, rather than a garden. No brown spaces or views. Maybe it's just the camera angles, Nick has started to mention it too, which as you know is most unusual, his engagement levels with gardening programmes being nil. Anyway it has inspired me to do a clear out. I have spent the last few days decimating the rockery – a scorched earth policy.

I know I have Nick, but sometimes I wish there was a slightly younger man on site. Not for eye candy, just arm candy, i.e., brawn. Nick could then do his best thing, telling him what to do and where to go, and I wouldn't have to struggle with heavy loads. I think everything would really move on apace. I would like to keep brawn man near at hand and at the ready. In fact the sooner they make a robot the better: my own gardening 'synth'. The more I think about it, *that* is the number one major gardening wish. He could be up the ladder, heaving the branches. I would watch and marvel – bliss and more bliss. He could live in the man shed. Nick would be happy to share and would love him too as I wouldn't be on the nag and he wouldn't need to worry about ladders and heights. Nick has spent the afternoon wiring up an intercom to the shed so communication won't be an issue.

I do know wishes and genies are a fraught combination. In literature anything involving a wish is doomed for disaster. Download *The Monkey's Paw* for more insight into this. Brawn man would probably lose a circuit and bludgeon Nick to death with the bulb planter, before tearing up the garden with the moss rake. (Hmm an idea for a sitcom: *The Good Life* meets *Shaun of the Dead*?)

I wish I could just relax and sit in the garden. The wood
recliners I bought at considerable cost are really just for show.
I think I have managed a rather jumpy ten minutes on one
of them. Lying down is an art form. There are three benches
positioned around the place in case I feel a bit weary and fancy a
stop off, but they are just set dressing too. Sometimes Bean and
I use them as workstations when we are doing useful things to
vegetables, and I have been known to perch on one to watch the
bird table but that's about it. Since my cataracts were sorted and
my vision is now akin to the red kite's, I can spot a weed from a
huge distance. There are sitters and there are jitterers. I am the
latter. I think you are too; I could put in a wish for both of us.

21

Minimum
in the Garden

I WOULD FORGIVE YOU if you had started to think that gardening is a bit of a mission. Before you send for the astro turf and concrete I thought I had better concentrate on what I consider to be the minimum amount you could do in a year. I haven't given up on the idea of training young Hendricks to do the gardening. He is a year now, so still malleable and open to suggestion.

When you take over the garden (I'm loving those words) the good news is that for the first year you can just do looking. Mow the lawn (obviously) and rake leaves in the winter, but really the best thing you can do is observe, and I mean *really* observe. Watch the seasons and see what emerges when. How does it look? When does it flower? How high does it grow? How long does it last? By looking you will see plants pushing up that you never even knew were there. This isn't being lazy, it's learning. Start to understand the basics. Once you have tweaked the seed heads off the daffodils or removed the dead leaves from the hellebores the process has started, you are about to surprise yourself by becoming a gardener. Some years life gets in the way, so in a busy year concentrate on basic maintenance in the garden. When the going gets quieter you can think about new projects and how you might progress them.

The year you got married I had to abandon all thoughts of gardening to become the director of a craft wedding industry, most of the components ending up in the house or round the cottage. I think the theme was 'simple in a field'. I am still recovering. The garden ended up with a few more weeds, a taller hedge and I felt a frisson of fraughtness whenever I looked round the beds, but the following year all was back to normal and nature continued on its course as though there had been no hiccup. It's possible to keep up quite a good veneer of control just by making sure the grass is cut and doing a bit of judicious deadheading. Deadheading is important. Nothing looks sadder than a rose with a cluster of brown petals. Deadheading also encourages plants to start flowering again and the leaves to regroup. If you do no other gardening task, do this one. The benefits are tangible and the garden will be given an instant lift. In a minimum year try to cut the hedges at least once – it will save time and energy in the long run. Chest height is favourite and then you can keep them neat by just cutting into soft new growth.

If life is becoming just too frenetic leave the vegetables (I can't believe I just wrote that). It is another area to cultivate and you can pick it up again the following year. Cover the ground with a piece of hideous black plastic if you want to suppress the weeds, or sow some green manure, which will build up the soil fertility until you do want to start planting. Maybe choose vegetables that really don't demand much work. Onions and garlic are simplicity itself and courgettes just go on producing (remember to cover them up while they are still at the plug stage). Nothing

inspires like a bit of success and I can promise strings of onions at the end of a season.

I am a huge fan of hardy geraniums. They are problem free. You do have to cut them back at the end of the season but that's it. Every year back they come, suppressing weeds and providing colour. They come in all shapes and sizes, tall and waving, small and spreading and each one is a pleasure. I don't think there is an easier plant in the garden. I am all for easy plants. There really is no point in fighting nature. Grow things that like our conditions – dry and chalky. In the past I have put in plants that would prefer to grow in marshland or the equivalent, but what is the point? I have usually had to take them out at a later stage when they just wouldn't do or, worse still, did a little bit.

Phone an expert. By that I mean the specialist growers. There are specialist growers for every type of plant from roses and geraniums through to agapanthus and pond plants. I have always found them help personified. Describe the conditions where the plant is going – shade, sun, chalk, etc. – tell them what colours you like and ask for advice. They absolutely know their products and whether it's a small company or a large one I have always found them more than happy to help. The key is that they must specialize and be masters in one area. This is a great time-saver, and you end up with varieties that you wouldn't have thought about, which should happily flourish where you plant them. To get the best advice, call them out of the season; by that time they're desperate for a chat.

Try not to make too many beds. I have just taken one back to grass. It was just too much work and not much to show for it. It took a couple of weeks to redistribute all the plants, but now it's done and I have put in a *Viburnum mariesii* shrub to bulk up instead. It is a palpable relief. I don't go in for bedding plants either. It does mean that at certain times of year the garden can look a bit bereft of colour, but can't we all?

Find a friend who loves to garden. It is nice to work alongside someone, and they can show you what's what. I have heard you burbling on about getting a gardener. Good luck with that one. I shall be watching out with interest to see how you get on. I don't like to say, 'forget it', but the fact is that most of the individuals who say they are gardeners aren't, they are really patio installers who can provide the odd shrub. They don't empathize with gardens. I know you think you can just call the expert. You could be lucky, but don't confuse hedge-cutting with plantsmanship. Bean may be on a zimmer by this time, but she will be happy to be wheeled over, advise and point. Pointing is very helpful.

22

Border Patrol
in the Garden

B Y GOVERNMENT STANDARDS (and indeed by
most garden standards) our borders are somewhat
porous. They are also, like the rest of the garden, an odd
mixture. There are wicker panels, shrubs, mixed hedging, and
sometimes absolutely nothing at all. Once upon a time granny
lived next door. This arrangement meant that borders weren't
an issue. There was a gap in the hedge, which allowed for the
traffic of small dogs and small you. Checks were not necessary
then, but life moves on and freedom of movement was curtailed.
Now the borders have been properly established although they
are still rather quaint. We suffer from higher ground syndrome;
the house next door is set several feet above us and so hedges
and fences are inclined to loom. The much hated leylandii
hedge is the dividing line (oh, that it were yew). Next door have
the best of it and indeed it actually looks rather smart from their
perspective. It can also be cut using a reasonably sized ladder,
with very little pain. From our side we crane our necks towards

the summit, wondering whether we have the bottle required to balance the ladder on the rockery for another season. You can't reach the top without performing this absolutely treacherous manoeuvre. The hedge is a definite candidate to cause the death of one or other of us.

The roof of the wood store is another moment when it would be a good idea to make peace with your maker. But that's gardening for you. Fact: an hour spent in the garden is more likely to result in injury than you cycling round Shoreditch (there are some rather good stats to do with garden disasters, the lawnmower causing the most injuries, hotly followed apparently by flower pots, make of that what you will).

Leylandii is also a hopeless specimen for a hedge in that it likes to truncate. This isn't a worry for next door but the view of legs shuffling past is depressing, especially when they aren't family legs. Bean came up with a really good idea for leg blocking, which was mini hazel hurdles, which we stuck in under the trees, but they have long rotted away and we need to start again. Apart from just looking awful, the hedge drains all the goodness from the local soil creating a dry bank, where something, but not much, will grow.

The other shrub that is encroaching over the border is laurel – a forest of the stuff. Every now and then I attack the branches that bash their way through to our side, blocking out the light and shedding large brown leathery leaves. Leylandii and laurel, what was the woman thinking of? Laurel is a very strong and elbows away at our wicker fence until it breaks through. It is huge now and as tall as the tree beside it. It needs a good thrashing with a chainsaw but it's not mine to thrash.

The new Hendricks Walk (I can't wait for him to use it) runs alongside the back border, which has been established with posts and wire. I have been training an ancient *Clematis montana* along the wire and I must say it is looking quite promising. It used to climb up into the laurel, and does grow to an astonishing height. Anyway, we cut it back to the ground and I started to twist it round the wire. It's made quite a hedge now, and I think may look rather beautiful when it flowers. It certainly looks as though something more interesting than nettles is happening at the back of garden, which is a major result.

The clematis leads on to a new addition: a row of *Sarcococca confusa*, or sweet box. This is supposed to be resistant to box blight, which is a horrid thing and many a box hedge has suffered from it. I hope topiary snail doesn't succumb. If you see brown dead leaves and a sort of dust, panic! Topiary snail has experienced many reincarnations and blight would be a sad ending. Sweet box smells sweet and has creamy white flowers followed by black berries. I hope it does well. It is planted in very unpromising soil, but that applies to most things in the garden. Note: it takes about three years for any shrub in our garden to really get going, so when you plant things and they don't romp straight off this is perfectly normal. If and when the box does get going, clip it to the height of the wire.

On the field side of the cottage, the border is even shakier. We have a mixed hedge that runs along for just a few metres with a small wooden gate that opens on to the field (most people would wonder why we need it). The gate came from the church. When the churchwardens commissioned a new one, the old gate was for the scrap heap but we have a fondness for a bit of old rubbish and recycled it to become field gate. We always go through it to access the field (although this is absolutely unnecessary due to the gaping holes along the border). Ted (the dog) likes to use the gate too. He thinks that is the proper way off the property, and will even wait for the gate to be opened before tearing off.

The small walnut tree on the border was grown from a nut. Squirrel had taken said nut from next door and buried it by the wall. I decided to replant it and it's quite a good height now with not too much of the Bankside lean to it. The huge sycamores beside it have self seeded and need to be thinned, and the larger walnut tree was a wedding present and seems to have survived being moved once, thrown on to the rubbish heap for a couple of months and then replanted, which is extraordinary. It is a fine tree now, although some years the leaves develop little polyps. Doctor's notes suggest leaf gall mite, which live on the underside of the leaves and cause the blisters. It doesn't seem to affect the walnuts, which is some comfort, but pretty it is not.

The front border, looking on to the road, has a cheering line of irises but grass is getting in the way and we need to decide whether to make a proper bed for them, or allow the plum saplings that pop up to develop into another hedge. The front border is being trashed by the huge combine harvesters that whizz up and down. They are too wide for the roads and it is only a question of time before we lose the wooden fence. The fence is one of the first things Nick built (and the reason for buying the fencing spade). A hedge would consolidate the bank, but the irises create their own sort of protection by waving out into the road so that cars slightly swerve to avoid them.

Back in the day when we had Porridge the Lhasa Apso, his favourite place to sleep on a hot day was on the bend of the road, the tarmac being rather cosy. The funny thing is there were so few cars then it really didn't matter. Now he would be a flat mat in thirty seconds. Lorries, vans, cars and cycle clubs have turned our quiet rural road into a heaving mass of metal. They won't slow down. Sometimes I like to do driver reminder by appearing in a surprising way round the hedge as they whizz past. A living speed bump! The postman likes to live life on the wild side too. He parks outside the front gate, yomping up the path before taking off again at breakneck speed. He is a man with no fear or no imagination, or maybe both. Walking to the pub requires nerves of steel, and don't get me started on the rubbish. Who are these people? Every country walk requires a carrier bag to collect coffee cups, sweet wrappers, tins and sandwich cartons. We are a nation of eaters and chuckers (I blame the parents).

The last bit of the border is a mixed hedge. Very mixed, with everything from gooseberry and plum to hawthorn and guelder rose (*Viburnum opulus*). Keep it to chest height. You could be naked and no one could see you, as this part of the garden is higher than the road. While I think of it, field maple makes a great hedge (we used it across the road) but it does take over. Anything else will be suffocated as it extends. Treat it ruthlessly, and you only ever need one or two to about six of anything else, even then I would put my money on the field maple to dominate.

So now you know the history of the borders. Keep them open. It is terribly friendly when neighbours pass by in their cars with a merry toot. Friends don't have to knock, they just appear in the garden, or hover for a quick chat en route. I would hate to live behind a stockade. Even if the natives were hostile I'd rather keep them in view. A few years ago as I was clearing up Christmas lunch in the kitchen, a very refined elderly lady appeared at my elbow by the sink demanding a gin and a packet of cigarettes. It appeared, she was drawn by the fairy lights around the door and thought we were the pub. I have never discovered who she was, but open borders make life more interesting.

23

Baring It
in the Garden

W HEN YOU NEED TO PLANT more hedging you will probably see the words 'bare-rooted'. This means that the plant will arrive without soil, just bare roots. Don't expect a flower pot! You should be armed and ready to plant, as they are supposed to go into the ground within a couple of days. If this isn't convenient then put them into a bit of earth until you are ready (heeling in). The idea behind the bare roots is the plants can rapidly adjust to their new conditions. Leave them in a bucket for a good drink before planting.

WHEN TO PLANT A HEDGE

Late autumn is a good time to get hedging. Hedges like spend the winter putting down roots, and they will be all the fitter for it. The recommended planting distance is 30-90 centimetres (1-3 feet) depending on how butch the plant is. I would go for

the latter as they do bulk up. To make use of the space stagger
the planting, putting the second plant slightly further back
than the first, the third going back in line with the first. Carry
on doing this so you create a double row and they appear rather
irregular when you look at them. This will make for a more
natural hedgerow. Water through the first year especially,
so they can get established. Buy online – there are hedge
specialists galore, and choose native species if you can, so they
blend in.

24

Overwintering
in the Garden

WINTER ALLOWS ME TO GIVE UP (I am good at giving up). I love the early nights, lighting candles and hunkering down. I do cosy. I am also rather keen on a deconstructed garden. Trees and shrubs reveal their shapes, leftover leaves are blackened from the first frosts and the garden is laid bare. There is a large patch of Japanese anemones by the shed which I like to leave as they really do look rather wonderful in their deadness, and the nude branches of the hazel becomes decorated with chaffinches that enjoy dangling from a tube of niger seeds. They took a long time to take up the challenge as the holes that pierce the plastic are minute, but just when I was about to throw in the seed they literally got the hang of it, now there is no stopping them.

I will give you the whole month off in December. Digging and delving can go on the back burner. But in late January on a sunny morning I can usually be found peering intently at the ground. I am on the watch for the first shoots to break through, panicking if they are too early, panicking if they are too late. Aconites with their chrome yellow petals are the first flowers to arrive. They are a shade of yellow I normally hate but at that time of year they work, shouting 'look at me' in a cheery voice. Early bulbs push out at the first sign of sunshine, as do the hellebores. The hellebore flowers will look prettier if you trim off any remaining leaves. I will already have given them one cutback at the end of the season, but there are always a few leaves remaining, and giving them a total clear-out allows the flowers to stand out, but I am getting ahead of myself.

Yes, I am one of those hideous people who actually enjoy Christmas. I know that some fear and loathe the season, but I like everything about it. It also works in the cottage. The cottage and Christmas are symbiotic. I have to say that after years of practice we have the whole event down to a fine art. The tree is bought from the local estate. They used to sell just a few, now it is an industry. We turn up the first weekend they are open. This is very important or you won't get the best shape. Of course there are thousands, but everyone knows there is only ever one tree with your name on it. We buy the Normandii, a six-footer. It scrapes the ceiling of the hall, and ever year Nick does his Scrooge and asks why we can't have a smaller tree? I ask you. We leave it outside – still wrapped in its net shroud until the week before Christmas, that way the branches have the best chance of staying upright.

The decorations have been collected over the years and are old friends. I can't resist buying a couple of new ones every year, but I especially love the miniscule wooden soldier you gave me as a Christmas present when you were about four. He is so small that sometimes he gets missed in the tissue paper and I scrabble about thinking he has been thrown out with the tree, but he always turns up.

Nick is in charge of wreath assembly. About twenty years ago he made a frame by twisting some hazel wands which he then adorned with greenery. Each year when it has done a turn, it goes back into the man shed to emerge the following year for Nick to resurrect. Some years he feels a bit minimalist (can't be asked) other years the wreath drips foliage (getting in touch with his feminine side). Nick does a lovely wreath. It knocks socks off the ones you see in the shops, which are far too constructed. It is one of his best things or, as he is fond of saying, 'just one of my best things'.

For the past few years I have grown just enough sprouts for Christmas lunch, and enough leeks to make a leek and potato soup for Boxing Day. This is another point to the vegetable garden. It adds to the Christmas traditions. Each year from about September we start sprout gazing and cogitate on whether we will have enough for the lunch. I actually count them, to work out the servings. I do love a sprout and I can't understand the antipathy some people have for them. They should be staked to keep them upright as they are inclined to become top-heavy, and they are best picked after the first frost, making them the ideal Christmas treat, so unless you have abandoned England for the Maldives, try to keep this tradition going.

Bringing the outside in also amuses me. There are little nails along the beam in the hall, so we can twist arborescent ivy along the wood. A bit like Nick and the wreath, some years barrow-loads of green stuff makes it inside, other years I do simple. As you know, I have never believed Christmas is for children. They haven't a clue about tree trimming and universally love tinsel. You were allowed a very small tree in your room to decorate with your stuff and I had mine. It proved an excellent learning experience as you are now an established member of the tree police. If you can't be a control freak a Christmas – well I give up.

There is usually a debate about putting lights up in the garden, but it does help guests up the path, so we tie small twinkly ones round the rose arch, and if we feel like going mad round the porch too. As you know, I do love a candle and would definitely get the path glowing, if someone could give me a method to keep them alight. Even on the stillest night they seem to blow out, regardless of every glass container I have tried.

Winters are definitely getting warmer. The primroses seem to flower right the way through the year now, not in the outrageous way they do round our way in spring, but you can always spot a few flowers that seem to keep on going. I underplanted the weeping pear and a *Viburnum* 'Mariesii' with white hardy cyclamen this year, and that has been a great success, drawing the eye to the dark patches. They kept on flowering for ages, right through to the end of February, giving very good value for very little effort (just what you want in winter). Primroses and snowdrops love our garden, which probably has something to do with the fact nobody eats them. Pheasants and pigeon consume every crocus I give them, but they don't touch the snowdrops, which is a major result, so we have a lot of them. I planted the first groups, but since then they have run amok seeding in every corner. We have mostly single snowdrops with a few patches of the double variety. I prefer the simplicity of the single ones. You simply can't feel gloomy when you look at a snowdrop, and you aren't required to do a thing to them. Mow round them until they have seeded and then mow over them.

Talking of mowing I had better give a mention to cowslips. They will appear in bulk all over the grass in the spring. Keep some patches, but mow over the tops of the rest or you will be starting to wonder where to walk. Which reminds me – winter is a good time to get the poor old mower and the tiller serviced. We usually don't, which means Nick has a challenging day with spanners and a tin of WD40.

25

Just Go for It
in the Garden

OVER WATER, UNDER WATER, plant them too close together or put them in upside down. The whole point of these ramblings is to inspire you to grasp a trowel and give it a go. Perhaps you would have liked more how-tos, but if you want the specifics on planting a potato there are plenty of books that address the basics, or you can just look it up on YouTube.

Considering how much effort I put in it is still remarkable how little I know. I know quite a bit about our garden but take me off piste and I would be looking round with the eye of a novice. In gardening you never stop learning, and the best way to learn about the garden is just to do it. You will get things wrong, but so do I. I am still working on the *Magnolia stellata* by the front gate. For some reason it just won't take off, and I had envisaged a statement bush . . .The garden has loads of areas that I have earmarked for improvement, which at certain times look rather bleak. It is a miraculous gardener who manages to keep the garden blooming at full tilt throughout the seasons.

Writing this made me realize that it is quite extraordinary how much pleasure I have got from this simple pursuit. It's not just the plants, it's the place, and how the cottage relates to the garden. Nick mentioned when we first started upgrading the hall, how important it was not to shut out the garden. So we put in the French windows and a stable door. Now on good days we can throw open the doors and we are just a foot away from plants. The top of the stable door can be left open on the more dismal days, just to let the air in and so I can absorb the view. It also makes the rooms appear larger, which in a cottage is a major plus as your eye is taken on to the green beyond.

'God dad' thought the title of Chapter 1 (Gardening From Beyond the Grave) rather gloomy. I have considered this and feel absolutely the reverse. I can think of nothing more positive as I wander around the plot, than to imagine it has a future, with the people I love creating their own stories and adventures in the garden. I see you have recently taken up house plants as a hobby. I am thrilled. I saw you considering one of them the other day, and thinking about its well-being and so I know that the journey has already begun.

Don't let the garden overwhelm you. It is easy to linger on all the things that are wrong, rather than the good bits. I am terrible for this, always thinking about the next job (if not the next three), so I am making a concerted effort to calm down. Revel in the month of June, when really you would have to own black fingers with orange spots for any garden not to perform. June is when all gardeners great and small think they must have done something right.

When you feel like putting your stamp on the garden (and you will). Start small. This will give you the confidence to have a go at larger projects. Just getting the pots up to speed will have you thinking that's it not such a mystery.

Wherever you are, start to look at plants. I was entranced by a small garden created on a railway station last year. Really, it was absolutely charming, the care and thought behind it was an inspiration. Even a trough by a gate can set you on a new planting path. I saw a huge glass conservatory in Cape Town which, rather than being filled with exotics, housed overscale hanging baskets, lined with sacking and filled with tumbling tomatoes. The beds underneath were awash with basil, the perfect pairing. That was it, nothing else and it provided me with a lesson that it doesn't have to be complicated to impress.

I just have this gut feeling that although you may run up the path into the cottage for the first couple of years, and probably just give a cursory glance to the rambling rose on the arch, there will come this moment. I see you stretched out on the sofa, fiddling with your iPad, when you glance up at the wall. A couple of flowers have fallen over, and there is a large dandelion or two taking up space. Curiosity will get the better of you and, like the proverbial moth, you will be drawn to get up and just take a look. Before you realize what is happening, you are tweaking at the leaves, which will lead you on to the man shed in a search for the secateurs . . . and by then, Calypso, it is all over, you have unwittingly just engaged with your garden. My love and enjoy.

Index

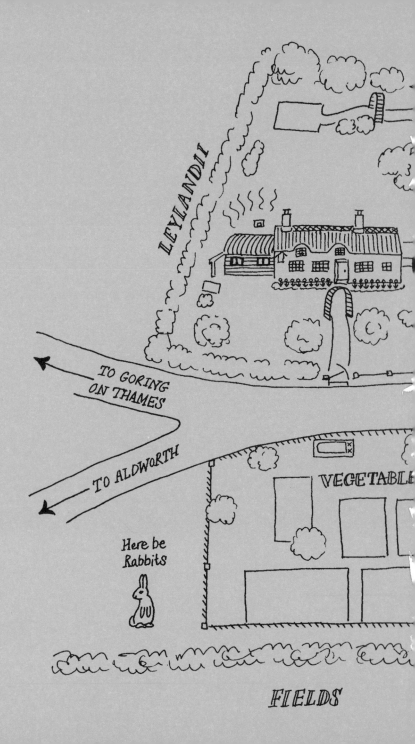